English
Olympiad

Class 03

A must have book for all
Olympiads & Talent Search Exams...

by
Dolly Jain

BL**O**OM CAP
Bloom Cap Edu Ventures Pvt. Ltd.

Bloom Cap Edu Ventures Pvt. Ltd.

✠ **Administrative & Production Office**

'Ramchhaya' 4577/15, Agarwal Road, Darya Ganj, New Delhi -110002
Tele: 011- 47630600, 43518550

✠ **ISBN :** 978-93-25519-22-0

✠ **PRICE :** ₹100.00

✠ **PO No :** TXT-XX-XXXXXXX-X-XX

For further information about the books log on to
www.bloomcap.org

Follow us on   

Preface

"Future belongs to those Who prepares for it today"

School Olympiads are National & International level competitions conducted by different Government, Non-Government & Educational Organisations with the purpose of making the children ready to face competitive exams.

The challenging Questions asked in Olympiads motivate them to learn more & more and bring out the best results with improved academic performance. The Awards & Scholarship offered by Olympiads motivate children to aspire & strive for doing better and emerge out to be the best.

English Olympiads

English is one of the most widely spoken languages across the world. In today's era, good command over English is considered as a must have skill. The greatest advantage of studying English is improvement in communication skills along with the growth of personality.

English Olympiads are meant to strengthen students' command over this universal language by improving spellings, grammar, sentence structure and to master student's language skills.

'Bloom English Olympiad Study Book Class 3' is a perfect resource to Study & Practice for Olympiad Exams and other National & State Level Talent Search Exams & Other Competitions.

Some Special Features of Bloom English Olympiad Study Books are;

- Complete coverage of all the aspects of English; Grammar, Reading Comprehension, Writing Skills, Spellings, Vocabulary & Communication Skills.
- Chapterwise Exercises having different types of Objective Questions at par with the Olympiad Level.
- Olympiad Pattern Practice Sets at the end.

This book is prepared by Expert Panel with the utmost care, still if you have any suggestions regarding its improvement then feel free to contact us at olympiads@bloomcap.org. We will try to inculcate your suggestions in the further editions.

Contents

Noun

Directions (Q. Nos. 1-8) Choose the type of noun of the underlined word in the sentences from the options given below.

1. The President will come to <u>India</u> after two days.
   (a) Common noun   (b) Proper noun
   (c) Collective noun   (d) Abstract noun

2. She will go to the <u>park</u> at 5:00 pm.
   (a) Material noun   (b) Collective noun
   (c) Abstract noun   (d) Common noun

3. <u>Honesty</u> is the best policy.
   (a) Abstract noun
   (b) Common noun
   (c) Material noun
   (d) Proper noun

4. The chairs and tables are made of <u>wood</u>.
   (a) Proper noun   (b) Collective noun
   (c) Material noun   (d) Common noun

5. I saw a huge <u>crowd</u> at the nearby mall.
   (a) Common noun
   (b) Proper noun
   (c) Collective noun
   (d) Abstract noun

6. Mala is the most intelligent <u>girl</u> in the class.
   (a) Masculine gender noun
   (b) Femine gender noun
   (c) Collective noun
   (d) Proper noun

7. The teacher asked the students to write down the notes in their <u>copies</u>.
   (a) Neuter gender noun
   (b) Masculine gender noun
   (c) Abstract noun
   (d) Material noun

8. The <u>boxes</u> are lying on the ground.
   (a) Material noun   (b) Plural noun
   (c) Singular noun   (d) Proper noun

Directions (Q. Nos. 9-13) Fill in the blanks with suitable noun.

9. Yesterday, I lost my .... of keys.
   (a) bouquet   (b) bundle
   (c) bunch   (d) packet

10. We saw a flock of .... on our way to home.
    (a) lion   (b) elephant
    (c) sheep   (d) tiger

11. .... gave me a bunch of grapes.
    (a) They   (b) She
    (c) He   (d) Shilpa

12. These flowers are made of ....
    (a) rug   (b) soil
    (c) paper   (d) pen

13. There is no .... in asking questions from the teachers.
    (a) loyalty   (b) shame
    (c) hunger   (d) sadness

Directions (Q. Nos. 14-17) Choose the correct abstract noun for the given word.

14. Kind

(a) Kindery

(b) Kindness

(c) Kindly

(d) Kindment

15. Wise

(a) Wisely   (b) Wiseness

(c) Wisdom   (d) Wisehood

16. Hungry

(a) Hungerness

(b) Hungered

(c) Hungriness

(d) Hunger

17. Bless

(a) Blessed   (b) Blesses

(c) Blessing   (d) Curse

Directions (Q. Nos. 18-21) Choose the option which is the correct example of the given word.

18. Countable noun

(a) Milk   (b) Oil

(c) Sugar   (d) Book

19. Uncountable noun

(a) Pen

(b) Table

(c) Milk

(d) Stick

20. Material Noun

(a) Ketchup

(b) Gold

(c) Paper

(d) Necklace

21. Common Noun

(a) City Hospital   (b) ABC School

(c) Country   (d) XYZ Restaurant

Directions (Q. Nos. 22-25) Read the words given below and identify their plural or singular form from the given options.

22. Buffalo

(a) Buffalos   (b) Buffales

(c) Buffaloes   (d) Buffalse

23. Shelf

(a) Shelfs   (b) Shelves

(c) Shelfes   (d) Shelfse

24. Heroes

(a) Heros   (b) Hero

(c) Herose   (d) Heroese

25. Stories

(a) Stori   (b) Storis

(c) Story   (d) Storise

Directions (Q. Nos. 26-30) Choose the correct opposite gender of the given word.

26. Emperor

(a) Emperoress   (b) Empriss

(c) Empress   (d) She emperor

27. Bull

(a) Vixen   (b) Cow

(c) Bullock   (d) Buffalo

28. Wife

(a) Husband   (b) Man

(c) Uncle   (d) Gentleman

29. Mare

(a) Deer   (b) Horse

(c) Pig   (d) Dog

30. Duchess

(a) Count   (b) Duch   (c) Duke   (d) Drake

Pronoun

Directions (Q. Nos. 1-12) Choose the correct pronouns to complete the sentences given below.

1. My brother loves to eat burgers. This burger is for ....
   (a) her   (b) them
   (c) him   (d) he

2. All my brothers love video games. Playing them is a favourite pastime of ....
   (a) their   (b) theirs
   (c) them   (d) ours

3. I paid for my scarf, so it is ....
   (a) mine   (b) yours
   (c) hers   (d) his

4. Hello, may I know .... is speaking?
   (a) which   (b) what
   (c) who   (d) whom

5. .... is the matter?
   (a) What   (b) Whose
   (c) Which   (d) Whom

6. My sister and I love sweets. These candies are for.......... .
   (a) her   (b) them
   (c) us   (d) me

7. Pick any of these desserts. The choice is ....
   (a) my   (b) yours
   (c) her   (d) him

8. These are my pets. I love ....
   (a) this   (b) them
   (c) we   (d) her

9. .... is my favourite doll?
   (a) Whose
   (b) Where
   (c) Whom
   (d) Which

10. I cannot lift this box. Could you help ...., please?
    (a) me   (b) him
    (c) her   (d) we

11. The Math book belongs to Ralph. It is ....
    (a) hers   (b) his
    (c) ours   (d) mine

12. .... are you going to invite?
    (a) What
    (b) Whom
    (c) Whose
    (d) Which

13. Match the nouns from List I with their pronouns from List II.

	List I		List II
A.	Kevin and Martin	1.	We
B.	Joseph	2.	It
C.	The box	3.	They
D.	Pat and I	4.	He

Codes

	A	B	C	D		A	B	C	D
(a)	3	2	1	4	(b)	4	3	1	2
(c)	3	4	2	1	(d)	1	3	2	4

14. Count the number of pronouns in the given box.

> He, Ram, Dog, She, We, Mother, They, Watch, His, The Earth, It, Her

(a) 10   (b) 7
(c) 12   (d) 4

Directions (Q. Nos. 15-19) Choose the correct demonstrative pronoun from the options given below.

15.

.... are delicious cookies.
(a) That   (b) This
(c) These   (d) Such

16.

.... is my house.
(a) These
(b) This
(c) Such
(d) Those

17.

.... are Raju's pencils.
(a) This   (b) Those
(c) That   (d) Such

18.

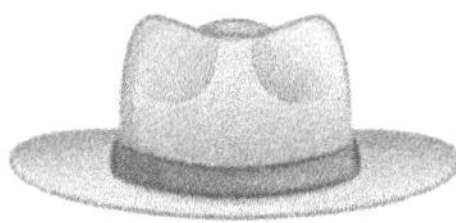

.... hat is mine.
(a) Those   (b) That
(c) These   (d) Such

19.

.... is Meera's bicycle.
(a) Such   (b) These
(c) Those   (d) This

Directions (Q. Nos. 20-24) Choose the correct option (noun) which is replaced by the underlined pronoun in the given sentences.

20. The boys were late, so the teacher scolded <u>them</u>.
(a) late   (b) the teacher
(c) scolded   (d) The boys

21. Kajal and Priya have a good teacher who advised <u>them</u> to work harder.
(a) Kajal and Priya   (b) good
(c) teacher   (d) harder

22. My name is Peter. <u>I</u> have come from America.
(a) America   (b) I
(c) Peter   (d) my

23. We have a computer at home, but we don't use <u>it</u>.
(a) we   (b) computer
(c) home   (d) use

24. Aahna is not good at Maths. I never take notes from <u>her</u>.
(a) Maths   (b) notes
(c) Aahna   (d) good

Directions (Q. Nos. 25 and 26) Read the given sentences and choose the option with the correct pronoun.

25. (a) Reema goes for shopping with her mother. **He** bought a new frock.
(b) Akash was uspset today. He lost **his** bag while coming home.
(c) The table is new. **She** is made of glass.
(d) Kaira cannot write properly. **They** need training.

26. (a) Shiva was a clever boy. **She** used to solve problems very quickly.
(b) My parents and **me** went to an amusement park yesterday.
(c) This parrot is so beautiful. **It** can talk as well.
(d) The Ganga is a holy river. **She** is worshipped by many people.

Directions (Q. Nos. 27-36) Given below is a story where some pronouns are missing. Read the story and fill in the blanks with correct pronouns.

Over a river there was a very narrow bridge. One day a goat was crossing this bridge. Just at the middle of the bridge he met another goat. There was no room for both of ...**(27)**... to pass.

"Go back," said one goat to the other, "There is no room for both of ...**(28)**...".

"Why should I go back ?", said the other goat. "Why should not you go back?"

"...**(29)**... must go back ", said the first goat, "because I am stronger than you."

"You are not stronger than ...**(30)**... ", said the second goat. "...**(31)**... will see about that ", said the first goat, and he put down his horns to fight.

"Stop!", said the second goat. "If we fight, we shall both fall into the river and be drowned. Instead I have a plan. ....**(32)**... shall lie down, and ...**(33)**... may walk over ...**(34)**.... ." Then the wise goat lay down on the bridge and the other goat walked lightly over ...**(35)**.... . So they passed each other and went on ...**(36)**... ways.

27. (a) him   (b) her
(c) them   (d) their

28. (a) me   (b) them
(c) us   (d) our

29. (a) I   (b) He
(c) You   (d) We

30. (a) me   (b) I
(c) them   (d) you

31. (a) They   (b) You
(c) We   (d) He

32. (a) Me   (b) You
(c) We   (d) I

33. (a) you   (b) we
(c) they   (d) he

34. (a) her   (b) me
(c) us   (d) his

35. (a) him   (b) her
(c) his   (d) their

36. (a) them   (b) their
(c) his   (d) yours

Verb

Directions (Q. Nos. 1-6) Fill in the blanks with suitable verbs.

1. He is .... the car very carefully.
   (a) shouting   (b) driving
   (c) honking   (d) walking

2. I .... at 10 p.m.
   (a) eats   (b) slept
   (c) plays   (d) sleeping

3. She is .... a poem in her book.
   (a) drawing   (b) making
   (c) writing   (d) catching

4. She .... loudly.
   (a) laughed   (b) made
   (c) baked   (d) roared

5. .... you need anything?
   (a) Was   (b) Do
   (c) Have   (d) Had

6. Shreya .... going to the park.
   (a) were   (b) is
   (c) did   (d) are

Directions (Q. Nos. 7-12) Identify the verbs in the given sentences.

7. Prakriti was reading a book.
   (a) was
   (b) reading
   (c) Both (a) and (b)
   (d) book

8. They have completed their work.
   (a) their
   (b) completed
   (c) work
   (d) they

9. He will not paint the wall.
   (a) he   (b) not
   (c) paint   (d) wall

10. We flew from New York to Australia.
    (a) we   (b) from
    (c) flew   (d) to

11. Mr Das was speaking very loudly.
    (a) Mr Das   (b) speaking
    (c) very   (d) loudly

12. John and Helen are at school.
    (a) and   (b) are
    (c) at   (d) school

Directions (Q. Nos. 13-17) Choose the option with the correct use of verb.

13. (a) Geeta likes to walk everyday.
    (b) Geeta likes to walk yesterday.
    (c) Geeta didn't likes to walk everyday.
    (d) Geeta will likes to walk tomorrow.

14. (a) They sang but didn't danced.
    (b) They sang but didn't do dance.
    (c) They sang but didn't dance.
    (d) They sang but didn't dancing.

15. (a) My brother takes out the trash.
    (b) My brother tooks out the trash.
    (c) My brother taken out the trash.
    (d) My brother take out the trash.

16. (a) Please told them the truth.
    (b) Please tells them the truth.
    (c) Please tell them the truth.
    (d) Please say them the truth.

17. (a) You could sleep here if you wants.
    (b) You can sleep here if you want.
    (c) You can sleep here if you wants.
    (d) You will sleep here if you wanted.

Directions (Q. Nos. 18-22) Choose the option with the incorrect use of verb.

18. (a) They played and wins the match.
    (b) I will talk to him myself.
    (c) He reached office but he didn't work.
    (d) We can go for a picnic.

19. (a) I am drawing a cat.
    (b) I should go out.
    (c) Sohan did not learnt his lessons.
    (d) Afsa is sleeping because she is not well.

20. (a) Tell me how it works.
    (b) Every child likes an ice-cream.
    (c) The children slid down the bank.
    (d) Do he play tennis?

21. (a) Tell me what happening?
    (b) My friend's dog barks a lot.
    (c) She doesn't use a computer.
    (d) Can you draw me a map of your street?

22. (a) I like to draw pictures.
    (b) I lent my sister some money.
    (c) A river flow through the valley.
    (d) I go to holiday every summer.

Directions (Q. Nos. 23-27) Given below are two sentences (A and B). State T (TRUE) for the sentence using verb correctly and F (FALSE) for the sentence using verb incorrectly.

23. Sentence A: Romans like to eat pizza.
    Sentence B: Seema is playing badminton.
    (a) FF   (b) TT
    (c) TF   (d) FT

24. Sentence A: Shalu is eat bread and butter.
    Sentence B: Kunal was waiting for his friend.
    (a) FT   (b) TT
    (c) TF   (d) FF

25. Sentence A: Jay ate the apple very fast.
    Sentence B: My canary singed songs.
    (a) TF   (b) FF
    (c) TT   (d) FT

26. Sentence A: It snow a lot in winter in Russia.
    Sentence B: She always forget her purse.
    (a) TT   (b) FF
    (c) TF   (d) FT

27. Sentence A: My uncle sang his son to sleep.
    Sentence B: I will go to England in order to improve my English.
    (a) FF   (b) FT   (c) TT   (d) TF

Adverb

1. The baby is sleeping ....
   (a) brightly   (b) peacefully
   (c) neatly   (d) slowly

2. The man is dressed ....
   (a) loudly   (b) early
   (c) neatly   (d) easily

3. The Sun is shining ....
   (a) peacefully   (b) frequently
   (c) already   (d) brightly

4. The milkman delivers milk ....
   (a) daily   (b) sadly
   (c) loudly   (d) neatly

5. The man is driving ....
   (a) unhappily   (b) suddenly
   (c) simply   (d) carefully

6. The musician plays ....
   (a) partly   (b) easily
   (c) melodiously   (d) hopefully

7. The jackal howls ....
   (a) quickly   (b) slowly
   (c) loudly   (d) brightly

8. I am confident as l am .... prepared for the exam.
   (a) enough   (b) fully
   (c) quite   (d) partly

9. Please park your car........ .
   (a) everywhere   (b) outside
   (c) behind   (d) forward

10. Kitty waited for the food ....
    (a) patiently   (b) easily
    (c) completely   (d) correctly

11. We ate food ....
    (a) sadly   (b) hungrily
    (c) beautifully   (d) softly

12. The water was .... cold.
    (a) extremely   (b) almost
    (c) fustly   (d) certainly

13. The taxi dropped us .... from the venue.
    (a) forward   (b) inside
    (c) under   (d) far away

14. Tina saw a lizard and ran out ....
    (a) loudly   (b) quickly
    (c) neatly   (d) angrily

15. The jar is kept .... the cupboard.
    (a) above   (b) here
    (c) away   (d) everywhere

16. My family will go to the museum today.
    (a) My family   (b) will go
    (c) museum   (d) today

17. Taj Mahal was built many years ago.
    (a) Taj Mahal   (b) built
    (c) ago   (d) years

18. He comes home very late.
    (a) He   (b) late
    (c) comes   (d) home

19. She completely forgot about his birthday.
    (a) forgot   (b) completely
    (c) birthday   (d) about

20. I learnt the chapters thoroughly.
    (a) learnt
    (b) chapters
    (c) thoroughly
    (d) I

Directions (Q. Nos. 21-24) Replace the underlined words with appropriate adverbs from the options given below.

21. The report on pollution came out <u>tomorrow</u>.
    (a) Day   (b) Ago
    (c) Yesterday   (d) Next day

22. We <u>neatly</u> got our grades from the test.
    (a) Boldly
    (b) Finally
    (c) Outside
    (d) Closely

23. I wasn't feeling well so I left Richa's party <u>late</u>.
    (a) Early   (b) Accidentally
    (c) Carelessly   (d) Deeply

24. The cat <u>softly</u> caught the mouse under his paws.
    (a) Later
    (b) Constantly
    (c) Legally
    (d) Swiftly

Directions (Q. Nos. 25-29) Read the passage given below. Fill in the blanks with adverbs to complete the passage.

Last night, Sohan had a ...(25)... sleep. In the morning, he woke up ...(26)... his alarm rang. He felt fresh and energetic. He dressed up ...(27)... . He could see the Sun shining ...(28)... from his window. His mother had prepared the breakfast ...(29)... and called him to come downstairs quickly. Sohan was rarely late for school.

25. (a) quickly   (b) everyday
    (c) sound   (d) slowly

26. (a) loudly   (b) before
    (c) partly   (d) very

27. (a) neatly   (b) soon
    (c) certainly   (d) never

28. (a) twice   (b) often
    (c) half   (d) brightly

29. (a) clearly   (b) already
    (c) beautifully   (d) daily

Directions (Q. Nos. 30 and 31) Given below are two sentences (A and B). State T (TRUE) for the sentence using adverb correctly and F (FALSE) for the sentence using adverb incorrectly.

30. Sentence A : He gently woke up the sleeping woman.

    Sentence B : The children love to play outside.
    (a) FF   (b) TF   (c) FT   (d) TT

31. Sentence A : The design certainly looks good on the paper.

    Sentence B : They were completely surprised by the snowfall.
    (a) TF   (b) FF
    (c) FT   (d) TT

Chapter 05

Adjective

Directions (Q. Nos. 1-6) Fill in the blanks with an appropriate adjective.

1. My shoes are really ...., so I need new ones.
   (a) slow   (b) weak   (c) old   (d) hard

2. His grandfather lost .... his wealth in the war.
   (a) most   (b) no
   (c) all   (d) whole

3. .... boy is very hardworking.
   (a) Those   (b) That
   (c) These   (d) Such

4. Radha is ill so she did not eat .... rice.
   (a) much   (b) any
   (c) all   (d) most

5. Nike does not like hot tea. He prefers .... milk.
   (a) full   (b) cold   (c) sour   (d) tasty

6. The queen is wearing a .... crown on her head.
   (a) ugly   (b) beautiful
   (c) golden   (d) Both (b) and (c)

Directions (Q. Nos. 7-10) Identify the noun for the underlined adjective.

7. They live in a <u>beautiful</u> house.
   (a) They   (b) house
   (c) live   (d) in

8. Hema is wearing a <u>sleeveless</u> shirt today.
   (a) shirt   (b) Hema
   (c) today   (d) wearing

9. My sister has <u>ten</u> dolls in her doll house.
   (a) my   (b) doll house
   (c) sister   (d) dolls

10. In the winter you must wear <u>woollen</u> clothes.
    (a) winter   (b) you   (c) wear   (d) clothes

Directions (Q. Nos. 11-15) Choose the adjective corresponding to the word given in capital.

11. DIRT
    (a) Dirtyful   (b) Dirtied
    (c) Dirty   (d) Dirtiable

12. LAUGH
    (a) Laughter   (b) Laughing
    (c) Laughable   (d) Laughed

13. ACHIEVE
    (a) Achievement   (b) Achievability
    (c) Achievable   (d) Achievity

14. ANGER
    (a) Angered   (b) Angerable
    (c) Angerment   (d) Angry

15. SUCCESS
    (a) Succeed   (b) Successfully
    (c) Successful   (d) Successibility

Directions (Q. Nos. 16-21) Identify the adjective in the following sentences.

16. The poor shoemaker worked hard to support his family.
    (a) shoemaker
    (b) support
    (c) poor
    (d) family

17. There are twenty apples in the basket.
    (a) there   (b) apples
    (c) basket   (d) twenty

18. She has many friends in Mumbai.
    (a) Mumbai
    (b) she
    (c) friends
    (d) many

19. Only a few students took the exam.
    (a) few   (b) too
    (c) exam   (d) students

20. He has a beautiful daughter.
    (a) He
    (b) beautiful
    (c) daughter
    (d) has

21. This ship will sail South tomorrow morning.
    (a) ship
    (b) This
    (c) tomorrow
    (d) morning

22. Choose the superlative degree of the word 'big'.
    (a) Big   (b) Bigger
    (c) More big   (d) Biggest

23. Choose the positive degree of the word 'hot'.
    (a) Hot   (b) Hotter
    (c) Hottest   (d) Most hot

24. Choose the comparative degree of the word 'happy'.
    (a) Happy
    (b) Happier
    (c) Most happy
    (d) Happiest

25. Choose the superlative degree of the word 'clean'.
    (a) Most cleanest   (b) Cleanest
    (c) Clean   (d) Cleaner

Chapter

06

Article

Directions (Q. Nos. 1-10) Fill in the blanks with a suitable article.

1. Iron is .... useful metal.
   (a) a   (b) an
   (c) the   (d) no article

2. .... Ganga is a sacred river.
   (a) A   (b) An
   (c) The   (d) No article

3. He is .... honourable man.
   (a) a   (b) an
   (c) the   (d) No article

4. Please give me........... hammer.
   (a) a   (b) an
   (c) the   (d) No article

5. .... Sun is very bright today.
   (a) A   (b) An
   (c) The   (d) No article

6. It takes me .... hour to reach home.
   (a) a
   (b) an
   (c) the
   (d) Either 'an' or 'the'

7. Please give me .... ice cream.
   (a) a   (b) an
   (c) the   (d) No article

8. Farukh is .... engineer.
   (a) the   (b) a
   (c) an   (d) None of these

9. What is .... name of the street?
   (a) the   (b) an
   (c) a   (d) No article

10. What did you have for .... lunch?
   (a) an   (b) the
   (c) a   (d) No article

Directions (Q. Nos. 11-13) See the given pictures carefully and choose the correct article that can be used with them.

11.

   (a) An   (b) A
   (c) The   (d) None of these

12.

   (a) An   (b) A
   (c) The   (d) None of these

13.

(a) An   (b) A
(c) The   (d) None of these

Directions (Q. Nos. 14-16) Choose the sentence with the correct use of article.

14. (a) Please give me orange.
    (b) Please give me a orange.
    (c) Please give me an orange.
    (d) Please give me the orange.

15. (a) It is honour to receive a medal.
    (b) It is a honour to receive the medal.
    (c) It is an honour to receive the medal.
    (d) It is the honour to receive a medal.

16. (a) Europe is smaller than Asia.
    (b) A Europe is smaller than Asia.
    (c) An Europe is smaller than Asia.
    (d) The Europe is smaller than Asia.

Directions (Q. Nos. 17 and 18) Answer the following questions with the help of words given in the box.

1. Largest	2. Himalaya
3. Orange	4. Umbrella
5. University	6. Incident

17. In the list given above, find out how many words will take the article, 'the'.

(a) 4   (b) 3   (c) 6   (d) 2

18. In the list given above, find out how many words will take the article 'an'.

(a) 3   (b) 1   (c) 4   (d) 2

Directions (Q. Nos. 19 and 20) Given below are two sentences (A and B). State T (TRUE) for the sentence using articles correctly and F (FALSE) for the sentence using articles incorrectly.

19. Sentence A : Tony got the first prize in the competition.

Sentence B : I need an glass of water.
(a) TT   (b) TF
(c) FT   (d) FF

20. Sentence A : I saw a one-eyed man in the circus.

Sentence B : He saw the doctor last week.
(a) TF   (b) FF
(c) FT   (d) TT

Directions (Q. Nos. 21-25) Read the passage given below. Fill in the blanks with articles to complete the passage.

Last month we went on a trip to ...**(21)**... Middle East. We travelled by ...**(22)**... plane to Cairo. Egypt is ...**(23)**... fantastic country. We saw pyramids and took ...**(24)**... boat tour on ...**(25)**... Nile.

21. (a) a   (b) an
    (c) the   (d) No article

22. (a) an   (b) a
    (c) the   (d) No article

23. (a) a   (b) an
    (c) the   (d) No article

24. (a) a   (b) an
    (c) the   (d) No article

25. (a) a   (b) an
    (c) the   (d) No article

Prepositions

Directions (Q. Nos. 1-5) Fill in the blanks with appropriate prepositions from the options given below.

1.

Some fruits are kept .... the basket.
(a) on   (b) in
(c) under   (d) over

2.

The books are .... the table and the chair.
(a) inside   (b) among
(c) between   (d) under

3.

A pile .... books is lying .... the table.
(a) of, on   (b) in, over
(c) of, under   (d) at, in

4. Birds are flying .... the sky .... the sea.

(a) in, over   (b) on, under
(c) by, above   (d) above, over

5.

The ball is .... the box ...... the floor.
(a) under, over   (b) behind, above
(c) near, on   (d) over, near

Directions (Q. Nos. 6-10) Choose the correct sentence according to the given picture.

6.

(a) The pig is under a sty.
(b) A pig is on a sty.
(c) A pig is in a sty.
(d) A pig is over a sty.

7.

(a) A pup is on a stool.
(b) A pup is in a stool.
(c) A pup is under a stool.
(d) A pup is over the stool.

8.

(a) A glass is beside the table.
(b) A glass is in the table.
(c) A glass is on the table.
(d) A glass is under the table.

9.

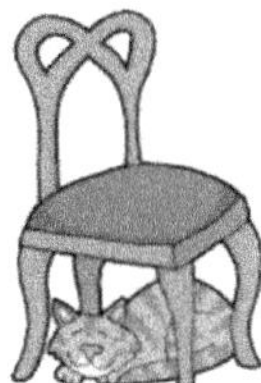

(a) The cat is sleeping behind the chair.
(b) The cat is sleeping next to the chair.
(c) The cat is sleeping under the chair.
(d) The cat is sleeping beside the chair.

10.

(a) Bees are flying at the flowers.
(b) Bees are flying in the flowers.
(c) Bees are flying over the flowers.
(d) Bees are flying around the flowers.

Directions (Q. Nos. 11-15) Identify the prepositions in the given sentences.

11. Her mother is a teacher in a reputed college.
(a) her   (b) a   (c) in   (d) is

12. The cow sat under the tree.
(a) the   (b) sat   (c) under   (d) tree

13. The keyboard is lying between the screen and the mouse.
(a) between   (b) mouse
(c) lying   (d) the

14. The Taj Mahal is situated on the banks of river Yamuna.
(a) situated   (b) of
(c) banks   (d) is

15. The plane is flying over the city.
(a) flying   (b) city
(c) the   (d) over

Directions (Q. Nos. 16-20) Choose the option which is not a preposition.

16. (a) With   (b) Among
(c) Either   (d) Above

17. (a) In   (b) At
(c) On   (d) Because

18. (a) Above   (b) Over
(c) Among   (d) And

19. (a) To   (b) Of
(c) In   (d) But

20. (a) Under   (b) Inside
(c) So   (d) Behind

Directions (Q. Nos. 21-30) Fill in the blanks with suitable prepositions from the options given below.

21. He came home ...... office.
(a) into   (b) from
(c) over   (d) with

22. His horse jumped ...... the fence.
   (a) over   (b) upon
   (c) down   (d) near

23. There is a gulf ...... the two cities.
   (a) through   (b) towards
   (c) between   (d) without

24. The kitchen is cleaned ..... Kirti.
   (a) to   (b) in
   (c) on   (d) by

25. He found the box ...... the table.
   (a) under   (b) above
   (c) below   (d) about

26. When will you arrive .... the office?
   (a) in   (b) to
   (c) at   (d) on

27. Kids are playing .... the garden.
   (a) outside   (b) in
   (c) above   (d) over

28. I think she spent the whole afternoon .... the phone.
   (a) in   (b) at
   (c) on   (d) over

29. I wake up ...... 7:00 a.m.
   (a) in   (b) on
   (c) at   (d) by

30. The child is hiding .... the door.
   (a) between   (b) behind
   (c) under   (d) above

Directions (Q. Nos. 31-35) Given below is a picture. Look at the picture and fill in the blanks by choosing the correct option.

31. The man is sitting .... an office chair.
   (a) in   (b) at
   (c) on   (d) over

32. The pile of books is .... the table.
   (a) on   (b) around
   (c) next to   (d) near

33. The books are .... the book case.
   (a) on   (b) in
   (c) at   (d) of

34. The cheese cake is kept .... the book case.
   (a) at   (b) above
   (c) on   (d) in

35. The picture is .... the wall.
   (a) in   (b) on
   (c) at   (d) up

Directions (Q. Nos. 36-40) Read the passage given below. Fill in the blanks with prepositions to complete the passage.

My family is going ...**(36)**... Agra. We will stay there ...**(37)**... our farmhouse. We are on a train. We started our journey ...**(38)**... Delhi. There are few stations ...**(39)**... Delhi and Agra. I am sitting ...**(40)**... the window. My parents are sitting behind me.

36. (a) in   (b) to
   (c) at   (d) since

37. (a) around   (b) over
   (c) in   (d) to

38. (a) from   (b) along
   (c) on   (d) upon

39. (a) towards   (b) between
   (c) near   (d) through

40. (a) near   (b) over
   (c) inside   (d) from

Conjunctions

Directions (Q. Nos. 1-5) Fill in the blanks with an appropriate conjunction.

1. John is a Canadian .... his wife is an Indian.
(a) since (b) or
(c) but (d) yet

2. It was raining .... I took an umbrella.
(a) and (b) because
(c) or (d) so

3. I could cook some dinner .... we could order some pizza.
(a) and (b) or
(c) but (d) so

4. I like fresh fruits .... not green vegetable.
(a) and (b) but
(c) yet (d) for

5. You can go to the tourist office .... ask for the information.
(a) and (b) because
(c) yet (d) but

Directions (Q. Nos. 6-10) Choose the conjunction in the given sentences.

6. The novel in English was long but very interesting.
(a) novel (b) long
(c) but (d) interesting

7. Paul and Claire like to swim.
(a) like
(b) to
(c) and
(d) Both 'a' and 'c'

8. She is kind so she helps people.
(a) she (b) is
(c) so (d) helps

9. The school bus driver wanted to turn right but had to turn left instead.
(a) bus driver (b) but
(c) turn (d) wanted

10. As I opened my eyes, I saw a strange sight.
(a) opened
(b) saw
(c) as
(d) I

11. Find out the number of conjunctions given in the box. Choose the correct answer from the options given below.

building	and	but	if
Sonam	or	Dr Sharma	table
so	for	because	church

(a) 5 (b) 6
(c) 7 (d) 9

Directions (Q. Nos. 12-16) Choose the option that correctly combines the given two sentences without changing their meaning.

12. Is that black? Is that white?
    (a) Is that black but white?
    (b) Is that black for white?
    (c) Is that black or white?
    (d) Is that black and white?

13. He is a genius. He is a lunatic.
    (a) He is both a genius and a lunatic.
    (b) If he is a genius or a lunatic.
    (c) He is a genius because he is a lunatic.
    (d) He is a genius yet he is a lunatic.

14. They cancelled the match. It rained.
    (a) They cancelled the match and it rained.
    (b) They cancelled the match but it rained.
    (c) They cancelled the match if it rained.
    (d) They cancelled the match because it rained.

15. A farmer sows a field. A farmer ploughs a field.
    (a) A farmer sows and ploughs a field.
    (b) A farmer sows or ploughs a field.
    (c) A farmer sows but ploughs a field.
    (d) A farmer sows so ploughs a field.

16. My computer was not working. I called a technician.
    (a) My computer was not working after I called a technician.
    (b) My computer was not working yet I called a technician.
    (c) My computer was not working because I called a technician.
    (d) My computer was not working, so I called a technician.

Directions (Q. Nos. 17-20) Choose the correct conjunction to combine the given sentences.

17. His father will be angry with him. He fought with his brother.
    (a) Yet   (b) So
    (c) Because   (d) Before

18. She is an intelligent girl. She is a hardworking girl.
    (a) Either…nor
    (b) Not only… but also
    (c) Hardly…than
    (d) Whether…or

19. I practice yoga daily. I couldn't put up a good show yesterday.
    (a) So   (b) Nor
    (c) For   (d) Yet

20. I wanted to play outside. I have to complete my homework.
    (a) I wanted to play outside and I have to complete my homework.
    (b) I wanted to play outside but I have to complete my homework.
    (c) I wanted to play outside since I have to complete my homework.
    (d) I wanted to play outside yet I have to complete my homework.

Directions (Q. Nos. 21-24) Given below are two sentences (A and B). State T (TRUE) for the sentence using conjunctions correctly and F (FALSE) for the sentence using conjunctions incorrectly.

21. Sentence A: I waited till the train arrived.
    Sentence B: Do you prefer tea and coffee?
    (a) FT   (b) TF
    (c) TT   (d) FF

22. Sentence A: It was cold since I shut the window.

Sentence B: Catch me if you can.

(a) FF   (b) TF

(c) TT   (d) FT

23. Sentence A: Alia is happy because she won the race.

Sentence B: Kanishk studied hard but failed the test.

(a) FF   (b) TT

(c) TF   (d) FF

24. Sentence A: He went out for it was raining.

Sentence B: He went to the hospital before he hurt his leg.

(a) FF   (b) FT

(c) TF   (d) TT

Directions (Q. Nos. 25-30) Given below is a dialogue between Mike and Peter with some blanks. Complete the dialogue by choosing the correct conjunction from the options.

Mike   Let's go out in the evening.

Peter   I'm sorry. I can't meet you today ...(25)... I'm busy. I can meet you tomorrow ...(26)... on Saturday.

Mike   Tomorrow I am busy ...(27)... I can't come. Is Saturday OK?

Peter   Sure, I am free all day, so let's go out!

Mike   Do you like flying?

Peter   No, I don't.

Mike   Why not?

Peter   ...(28)...   I can't sleep well ...(29)... airports are really boring.

Mike   Right. The first time airports are really exciting ...(30)... , then they lose their charm and become boring.

Peter   OK, then we are meeting on Saturday.

Mike   Oh sure!

25. (a) as   (b) because

(c) for   (d) All of these

26. (a) and   (b) or

(c) nor   (d) yet

27. (a) yet   (b) but

(c) so   (d) and

28. (a) Because   (b) but

(c) so   (d) or

29. (a) or   (b) and

(c) so   (d) because

30. (a) and   (b) but

(c) or   (d) so

Sentence and Its Types

Directions (Q. Nos. 1-4) Identify the subject in the following sentences.

1. The young lady sat under a tree.
(a) The young
(b) The young lady
(c) sat
(d) under a tree

2. Next week my father is coming from Japan.
(a) Next week
(b) my father is coming
(c) my father
(d) coming from Japan

3. Rehman won a medal.
(a) Rehman
(b) won a medal
(c) a medal
(d) Rehman won

4. Mina is writing a letter to her father.
(a) Mina is
(b) Mina
(c) is writing
(d) to her father

Directions (Q. Nos. 5-8) Identify the predicate in the given sentences.

5. My father drives his car.
(a) drives
(b) My father
(c) drives his car
(d) car

6. A good child never tells a lie.
(a) A good child
(b) never tells a lie
(c) never tells
(d) a lie

7. The Himalayas is the highest mountain range.
(a) The Himalayas
(b) is the
(c) highest mountain range
(d) is the highest mountain range

8. Tina and her friends went to the movies.
(a) Tina and her friends
(b) Went to the movies
(c) Tina
(d) Tina and her friends went

9. Match the following subjects with their predicates.

List I (Subject)	List II (Predicate)
A. Laughter	1. is my favourite teacher.
B. Ms Teena	2. created all of us.
C. Children	3. is the best medicine.
D. God	4. like to play.

Codes

	A	B	C	D			A	B	C	D
(a)	1	2	3	4		(b)	3	1	4	2
(c)	4	2	1	3		(d)	2	1	4	3

Directions (Q. Nos. 10-13) Fill in the blank to form a meaningful sentence.

10. I invited Ruby to my party. She did not accept ....
    (a) the problem
    (b) the invitation
    (c) the work
    (d) the performance

11. Can you not solve .... ?
    (a) that offer   (b) the answer
    (c) this problem   (d) some money

12. Mother cut the cheese ....
    (a) with a fork   (b) with a knife
    (c) with spoon   (d) with scissors

13. Those dresses used to ....
    (a) be my   (b) be mine
    (c) be me   (d) be I

Directions (Q. Nos. 14-17) Change the given sentences as directed.

14. Change into negative sentence.
    I want to go to Europe for vacations.
    (a) Do I want to go to Europe for vacations?
    (b) I do not want to go to Europe for vacations.
    (c) Go to Europe for vacations.
    (d) Both (b) and (c)

15. Change into interrogative sentence.
    I want to have some milk.
    (a) Don't you want milk?
    (b) Do you want to have some milk?
    (c) Do you want to drink milk?
    (d) I do not want milk.

16. Change into imperative sentence.
    You should not break the rules.
    (a) Break the rules, please.
    (b) Please! Break the rules.
    (c) Don't break the rules.
    (d) You shouldn't break the rules.

17. Change into exclamatory sentence.
    He is a very intelligent boy.
    (a) He is what an intelligent boy!
    (b) What an intelligent boy he is!
    (c) How an intelligent boy he is!
    (d) An intelligent boy he is!

Directions (Q. Nos. 18-20) Do as directed and choose the correct option for the given sentences.

18. Identify the interrogative sentence.
    (a) Wow! my mother is a doctor!
    (b) My mother is a doctor.
    (c) Is my mother a doctor?
    (d) None of the above

19. Identify the negative sentence.
    (a) I will go to school today.
    (b) I will not go to school today.
    (c) Will I go to school today?
    (d) I will go to school today!

20. Identify an exclamatory sentence.
    (a) I am so excited.
    (b) Am I so excited?
    (c) I am so excited!
    (d) I am not so excited.

21. Match the sentences given in List I with their types in List II.

	List I		List II
A.	Why didn't you come to school today?	1.	Assertive
B.	Please pass the salt.	2.	Interrogative
C.	I love you so much!	3.	Imperative
D.	I am ten years old and love my school very much.	4.	Exclamatory

Codes

	A	B	C	D
(a)	3	2	1	4
(b)	2	3	4	1
(c)	1	4	2	3
(d)	2	1	4	3

Directions (Q. Nos. 22-24) The given sentences are broken into subject and predicate. Identify the correct sentences.

22. A. The sun/ was shining brightly.
    B. The dogs/ were barking loudly.
    C. The pretty girl was wearing/ a blue frock.
    D. My younger brother serves in/ the army.

    Codes
    (a) A and C
    (b) B and D
    (c) A and B
    (d) B and C

23. A. The man and his wife were working in their /garden.
    B. My mother and my aunt/ are trained classical dancers.
    C. The train/ left the station.
    D. A dog was chasing/ a boy.

    Codes
    (a) A and D
    (b) B and C
    (c) A and B
    (d) C and D

24. A. My students always do/their work.
    B. He/has a huge house.
    C. The soup tastes/good.
    D. They/are watching a horror film.

    Codes
    (a) B and D
    (b) B and C
    (c) A and C
    (d) C and D

Directions (Q. Nos. 25 and 26) Read the given sentences and mark the correct sentence as True (T) and incorrect sentence as False (F).

25. Sentence A : Sam and his dog (sub)/ ran on the beach. (pre)

    Sentence B : Mr. Hansen (sub)/ teaches the class. (pre)

    (a) TT   (b) FF
    (c) FT   (d) TF

26. Sentence A : Zaid was puzzled (sub)/ with the complicated math problem. (pre)

    Sentence B : Dev's mother (sub)/ didn't let him do anything. (pre)

    (a) TF   (b) FF
    (c) FT   (d) TT

Directions (Q. Nos. 27 and 28) Answer the following questions.

> Rahul, are going to Kanpur, They, is eating sugar, We, The doctor, Lion, She, The dolphin, is running on the beach, is roaring. His mother, is parked outside, My car, is cooking, are dancing, A big lizard, lives in a jungle, was crawling

27. Count the number of subjects in the given box.
    (a) 10   (b) 9
    (c) 15   (d) 11

28. Count the number of predicates in the given box.
    (a) 8   (b) 9
    (c) 15   (d) 18

Chapter 10

Tense

Directions (Q. Nos. 1-14) Fill in the blanks with correct tense form according to the sentence.

1. She usually ……. the newspaper in the evening.
   (a) read   (b) reads
   (c) reading   (d) readed

2. I ……. the cups. You can dry them.
   (a) is washing   (b) shall wash
   (c) was washed   (d) are washing

3. They ……. a movie every Saturday.
   (a) watch   (b) watches
   (c) watched   (d) watching

4. My grandfather ………… tea every morning.
   (a) cook   (b) drinking
   (c) takes   (d) having

5. The policeman ……. the thief red handed.
   (a) catching   (b) caught
   (c) is catch   (d) is caught

6. James ……. the vase in anger.
   (a) breaks   (b) broken
   (c) broke   (d) breaked

7. They ……. singing everyday.
   (a) practiced   (b) practices
   (c) practice   (d) practicing

8. We ……. the problem because the teacher explained it well.
   (a) understand
   (b) understands
   (c) understood
   (d) understanding

9. My mother generally ……. delicious food.
   (a) cook   (b) cooked
   (c) cooking   (d) cooks

10. My father ……. a new house next year.
    (a) will buy   (b) is bought
    (c) was bought   (d) are buying

11. The Sun ……. in the East.
    (a) rise   (b) rises
    (c) rose   (d) rised

12. Susan ……. at 3 o'clock tomorrow.
    (a) will come   (b) was coming
    (c) shall coming (d) is coming

13. The farmer ……. money from the moneylender yesterday.
    (a) borrows   (b) borrow
    (c) borrowed   (d) borrowing

14. The cat ……. from the table to catch the rat.
    (a) jump   (b) is jump
    (c) jumped   (d) jumping

Directions (Q. Nos. 15-19) Change the tense of the underlined verb as directed.

15. Change the tense into simple past tense.

She <u>wakes up</u> early in the morning.
(a) wake up   (b) woke up
(c) waking up   (d) waked up

16. Change the tense into simple future tense.

The teacher <u>is delivering</u> the lecture.
(a) will deliver   (b) will delivers
(c) will delivered   (d) will delivering

17. Change the tense into past continuous.

He <u>works</u> in this hotel as a chef.
(a) worked   (b) working
(c) was working   (d) was worked

18. Change the tense into present continuous tense.

He <u>admired</u> the poetry of Shakespeare.
(a) admire   (b) will admire
(c) admiring   (d) is admiring

19. Change the tense into future continuous tense.

I <u>was playing</u> basketball the whole evening.
(a) will play   (b) will playing
(c) will be playing   (d) will played

20. Match the following sentences given in the List I with the type of tense used in List II.

List I		List II
A.	He is walking to the door.	1. Simple Present Tense
B.	I will go to the beach next Sunday.	2. Present Continuous Tense
C.	I was peeling potatoes in the kitchen yesterday.	3. Past Continuous Tense
D.	I speak French quite well.	4. Simple Future Tense

Codes

	A	B	C	D		A	B	C	D
(a)	1	2	3	4	(b)	2	4	3	1
(c)	3	4	1	2	(d)	2	1	3	4

Directions (Q. Nos. 21-24) Fill in the blanks with Past, Present and Future Continuous tense form of the verbs.

21. Sita .... from fever last week.
(a) will suffer   (b) was suffering
(c) had suffering   (d) were suffering

22. The light went out while they .... dinner.
(a) having   (b) are having
(c) were having   (d) will have

23. The police van .... the streets.
(a) is patrolling   (b) were patrolling
(c) are patrolling   (d) patrolling

24. Jack and Ronny .... the tennis match on TV.
(a) will be watching
(b) was watching
(c) is watching
(d) watch

Directions (Q. Nos. 25 and 26) Identify the tense of the following sentences by the underlined words.

25. He fell asleep while he <u>was driving</u>.
(a) Present Continuous tense
(b) Simple Present tense
(c) Past Continuous tense
(d) Simple Future tense

26. Why <u>aren't you doing</u> your homework?
(a) Simple Present tense
(b) Past Continuous tense
(c) Present Continuous tense
(d) Future Continuous tense

Chapter 11

Punctuation

Directions (Q. Nos. 1-5) Fill in the blanks with the correct punctuation mark to make meaningful sentences.

1. Do you know where is Ram ....
   (a) .   (b) ?
   (c) !   (d) ,

2. Wow .... Look at the fireworks.
   (a) !   (b) ?
   (c) .   (d) ;

3. Sara ate pizza for lunch ....
   (a) -   (b) ?
   (c) .   (d) !

4. I purchased an apple .... banana and a mango.
   (a) ,   (b) !
   (c) :   (d) ?

5. Long live the king ....
   (a) ,   (b) !   (c) .   (d) :

Directions (Q. Nos. 6-10) Choose the option which correctly punctuates the given sentence.

6. apples Mangoes and bananas are my favourite?
   (a) apples, mangoes and bananas are my favourite.
   (b) Apples; Mangoes; and Bananas are my favourite.
   (c) Apples, Mangoes and bananas : are my favourite!
   (d) Apples, mangoes and bananas are my favourite.

7. he was honest; sincere; and hardworking.
   (a) He was Honest, sincere, and Hardworking?
   (b) He was : honest, sincere, and hardworking!
   (c) He was honest, sincere and hardworking.
   (d) He was honest, sincere and : hardworking.

8. hindus muslims Sikhs christians live together in india
   (a) Hindus muslims Sikhs christians live together in India
   (b) Hindus, Muslims, Sikhs and Christians live together in India.
   (c) Hindus Muslims Sikhs Christians live together in India.
   (d) hindus muslims Sikhs christians live together in India.

9. my friend priya speaks german
   (a) My friend priya speaks german.
   (b) my friend Priya speaks german.
   (c) My friend Priya speaks German.
   (d) My friend Priya speaks german

10. akbar the greatest of the mughal emperors rules wisely
    (a) Akbar, the greatest of the mughal emperors ruled wisely.
    (b) Akbar, the greatest of the Mughal emperors ruled wisely.
    (c) Akbar the greatest of the Mughal Emperors ruled wisely.
    (d) Akbar, the greatest of the Mughal emperors, ruled wisely.

Directions (Q. Nos. 11-16) Find the sentence with correct punctuations.

11. (a) How long will you be gone!
    (b) How long will you be gone?
    (c) How long will you be gone.
    (d) How long will you be gone;

12. (a) Miss Benny? May I use your telephone?
    (b) Miss Benny! May I use your telephone!
    (c) Miss Benny, May I use your telephone?
    (d) Miss Benny, May I use your telephone.

13. (a) Bill added, they are eating all the peanuts.
    (b) Bill added they are eating all the peanuts?
    (c) Bill added. they are eating all the peanuts.
    (d) Bill added, "They are eating all the peanuts".

14. (a) The fruit seller sells apples oranges mangoes etc.
    (b) The fruits seller sells apples, oranges, mangoes, etc.
    (c) The fruit seller sells apples; oranges; mangoes etc.
    (d) The fruit seller, sells apples mangoes etc.

15. (a) Alas! What a terrible fire!
    (b) Alas. What a terrible fire.
    (c) Alas, what a terrible fire!
    (d) Alas; what a terrible fire

16. (a) Hardwork honesty and self-confidence lead to success.
    (b) Hardwork, honesty and self-confidence lead to success.
    (c) Hardwork, honesty, self-confidence, lead to success.
    (d) Hardwork, honesty, self-confidence lead to success?

Directions (Q. Nos. 17-21) Select the sentence which is punctuated incorrectly.

17. (a) Nick will reach Delhi on Friday.
    (b) He will visit the Red fort Qutub Minar Raj Ghat Chandni Chowk.
    (c) Red Fort, Qutub Minar and Chandni Chowk are located in Central Delhi.
    (d) Nick asked, "How far is Qutub Minar from Central Delhi?"

18. (a) Summer, winter, autumn and spring are the four main seasons.
    (b) Each season has its unique charm.
    (c) In the spring season flowers blossom fresh leaves grow its lush green everywhere.
    (d) Leaves become orange and yellow during autumn.

19. (a) Alas The great poet is no more.
    (b) He suffered from cancer.
    (c) The loss is great!
    (d) His poems, stories and letters are widely read.

20. (a) Sam woke up in the morning.
    (b) He said, "What a lovely day!"
    (c) He had to go to school.
    (d) He had not finished his maths science english homework.

21. (a) My mother is cooking dinner.
    (b) She needs butter, rice, flour, etc.
    (c) She asked me, "Where is the jam?"
    (d) I said I do not know.

22. Match the sentences in List I with appropriate punctuation marks in List II.

	List I		List II
A.	Could you please give me that book	1.	(!)
B.	This is extraordinary	2.	(.)
C.	My aunt will come tomorrow	3.	(?)
D.	I ordered a pizza a burger and some chips.	4.	(,)

Codes

	A	B	C	D
(a)	3	1	2	4
(b)	1	3	4	2
(c)	3	2	1	4
(d)	2	3	4	1

Directions (Q. Nos. 23-29) Given below is a paragraph which is without the use of punctuation marks. Read the paragraph and use comma, exclamation mark, question mark and full stop where required.

I have a dog ...**(23)**... He is a labrador. He is black in colour ...**(24)**... has big ears and a long tail. He wags his tail and licks my face when he is happy ...**(25)**... He loves going for walks. I take him to school sometimes. He is friends with a bulldog ...**(26)**.... a german shepherd and a pug ...**(27)**... Once he saw a black cat and wanted to chase her too.

O Lord ! He is as swift as an eagle ...**(28)**... He also likes to look at the children playing in the garden ...**(29)**... I wish I could spend all my time with him.

23. (a) (?)   (b) (.)   (c) (,)   (d) (!)

24. (a) (.)   (b) (,)   (c) (!)   (d) (;)

25. (a) (!)   (b) (,)   (c) (?)   (d) (.)

26. (a) (.)   (b) (!)   (c) (?)   (d) (,)

27. (a) (,)   (b) (!)   (c) (.)   (d) (?)

28. (a) (!)   (b) (?)   (c) (.)   (d) (,)

29. (a) (,)   (b) (!)   (c) (.)   (d) (?)

30. Count the number of punctuation marks in the given box.

(.)	(%)	($)	(" ")	
(?)	(#)	(@)	(!)	(*)
(^)	(&)	(,)	(:)	(G)

(a) 9   (b) 6

(c) 14   (d) 10

Jumbled Words and Sentences

Directions (Q. Nos. 1-20) Unscramble the alphabets to form meaningful words.

1. TKSIANG
   (a) Skeeing   (b) Skating
   (c) Skipping   (d) Skiing

2. CKTIHNE
   (a) Tiknitch   (b) Chicken
   (c) Kitchen   (d) Kitten

3. PTERMOCU
   (a) Compacter   (b) Computer
   (c) Pomcuret   (d) Morpetcu

4. IDNIGV
   (a) Driving   (b) Winning
   (c) Giving   (d) Diving

5. RIKCETC
   (a) Ticker   (b) Ticket
   (c) Cricket   (d) Wicket

6. LWOBIGN
   (a) Gobling   (b) Bating
   (c) Bowling   (d) Gliding

7. NGOEDL
   (a) Noegde
   (b) Longed
   (c) Dongle
   (d) Both (b) and (c)

8. BOFTOALL
   (a) Volleyball   (b) Football
   (c) Baseball   (d) Ball

9. RASIMLI
   (a) Rasmili   (b) Similar
   (c) Misalir   (d) Misilar

10. UGBRER
    (a) Rubber   (b) Burger
    (c) Rubger   (d) Grubber

11. REPTYT
    (a) Terry   (b) Party
    (c) Pretty   (d) Plenty

12. RHEBOTR
    (a) Broth   (b) Robot
    (c) Bother   (d) Brother

13. GIHNKI
    (a) Biking   (b) Hiking
    (c) Viking   (d) Niking

14. LEPCNI
    (a) Lentil   (b) Pencil
    (c) Lipcen   (d) Pilenc

15. OXNBIG
    (a) Bignox   (b) Bowling
    (c) Balling   (d) Boxing

16. CRIUOSU

   (a) Ricusuo   (b) Suricou

   (c) Curious   (d) Ouricus

17. LACHYPSI

   (a) Laphysic   (b) Physical

   (c) Shypical   (d) Hypicals

18. OCRENR

   (a) Orcner   (b) Ronerc

   (c) Corner   (d) Norrec

19. KANPIN

   (a) Napkin   (b) Kapnin

   (c) Pankin   (d) Apnikn

20. SCOEDL

   (a) Dolecs   (b) Sloced

   (c) Losedc   (d) Closed

Directions (Q. Nos. 21-40) Rearrange the words to form meaningful sentences.

21. Many/ garden / there / in / plants/ are /the.

   (a) Many plants there are in the garden.

   (b) There are many plants in the garden.

   (c) There are plants in the many garden.

   (d) There are many garden in the palnts.

22. Run/ I / morning / miles / every/ four.

   (a) I run four miles every morning.

   (b) Run four I every morning miles.

   (c) Every four miles I run morning.

   (d) Every miles run I four morning.

23. Rises/ the Sun / the / East / in/ West/in/ the/ sets/ and.

   (a) The Sun in rise the East and the West sets in.

   (b) The Sun rises in the East and sets in the West.

   (c) The Sun rises East in the and West in the sets.

   (d) The rises Sun in the East and West in the sets.

24. boy / is / an / the / eating / apple.

   (a) Eating an the apple is boy.

   (b) The boy is eating an apple.

   (c) The boy eating an apple is.

   (d) An apple is eating the boy.

25. play / every day / cricket / we.

   (a) Play cricket we everyday.

   (b) Everyday cricket we play.

   (c) We play cricket every day.

   (d) Play everyday we cricket.

26. is / medicine / laughter / best / the.

   (a) Laughter is the best medicine.

   (b) Medicine is the best laughter.

   (c) Best laughter is the medicine.

   (d) The best medicine is laughter.

27. shines / the / day / during / Sun / the.

   (a) The day shines during Sun the.

   (b) Shines the day during the Sun.

   (c) The Sun during shines the day.

   (d) The Sun shines during the day.

28. Homework / almost / my / is / complete.

   (a) My homework is almost complete.

   (b) Homework is almost complete my.

   (c) My almost homework complete is.

   (d) My homework is complete almost.

29. Flowers / everywhere / there / are / the spring / during.

   (a) The spring there are everywhere flowers.

   (b) During the flowers there are spring everywhere.

   (c) Spring are there flowers during everywhere.

   (d) There are flowers everywhere during the spring.

30. free/time/ with / little / left/ her / her/ job.

   (a) Her little free time job left her with.

   (b) Her job time left her with little free.

   (c) Her job left her with little free time.

   (d) Her job left her with free time little.

31. Piano / school / have / I / practice / after.
    - (a) I have piano practice after school.
    - (b) I have school practice after piano.
    - (c) I have piano after school practice.
    - (d) I have practice after school piano.

32. You / can / blue / the / bike / ride?
    - (a) Can you bike the ride blue?
    - (b) You can ride the bike blue?
    - (c) Can you ride the blue bike?
    - (d) You can ride the blue bike?

33. Decided / has / new / a / buy / computer / he / to.
    - (a) He decided a new computer has to buy.
    - (b) He has decided to buy a new computer.
    - (c) He has to buy a new computer decided.
    - (d) He has decided a new computer to buy.

34. I / the / prize / won / in / the / quiz / competition / first.
    - (a) I the won prize first in the quiz competition.
    - (b) I won the first prize in the quiz competition.
    - (c) I won the first competition in the quiz prize.
    - (d) I the first prize won in the competition quiz.

35. My / are / us / cousins / next / visiting / month.
    - (a) My cousins visiting us are next month.
    - (b) Month us next my cousins visiting are.
    - (c) My cousins are visiting us next month.
    - (d) Cousins are visiting us next month my.

36. Reading / an / am / I / interesting / now / story.
    - (a) I am reading an interesting story now.
    - (b) Reading I am an interesting story now.
    - (c) I am an interesting story reading now.
    - (d) I am an interesting reading story now.

37. The / I / have / all / questions / answered.
    - (a) The questions I have answered all.
    - (b) I have questions all the answered.
    - (c) The answered questions all I have.
    - (d) I have answered all the questions.

38. The / I / going / Saturday / am / zoo / to / on.
    - (a) On the Saturday going I am to zoo.
    - (b) On the zoo, I am going to Saturday.
    - (c) I am to the zoo going on Saturday.
    - (d) I am going to the zoo on Saturday.

39. Sat / she / beautiful / room / in a / and / big.
    - (a) She in a big and beautiful room sat.
    - (b) She sat in a big and beautiful room.
    - (c) In a big beautiful room and she sat.
    - (d) In a big and beautiful room sat she.

40. I / to / become / like / a / writer / I / grow / up / when / would.
    - (a) When I grow up, I would to become a writer like.
    - (b) I would become a writer when I like to grow up.
    - (c) When I become to a writer I would like grow up.
    - (d) I would like to become a writer when I grow up.

Chapter 13

Synonyms

Directions (Q. Nos. 1-6) Find the synonym of the given words. Choose the correct answer from the given options.

1. Alien

  (a) Native   (b) Common

  (c) Tenant   (d) Foreigner

2. Bounce

  (a) Walk   (b) Jump

  (c) Lie down   (d) Stand

3. Shy

  (a) Bright   (b) Energetic

  (c) Quiet   (d) Tiny

4. Terrible

  (a) Sweet   (b) Incredible

  (c) Horror   (d) Horrible

5. Charming

  (a) Right   (b) Attractive

  (c) Sorrow   (d) Incorrect

6. Innocent

  (a) Fair   (b) Blame

  (c) Foolish   (d) Honest

Directions (Q. Nos. 7-12) Choose the synonym of the underlined words.

7. He gifted me a very <u>expensive</u> watch.

  (a) cheap

  (b) costly

  (c) huge

  (d) shiny

8. Jack is a <u>laborious</u> boy.

  (a) smart   (b) energetic

  (c) hard-working   (d) happy

9. I don't <u>remember</u> where I met Kate.

  (a) shallow   (b) forget

  (c) analyse   (d) recall

10. The show was very <u>entertaining</u>.

  (a) dull   (b) funny

  (c) enjoyable   (d) boring

11. The sum was <u>difficult</u>.

  (a) tight   (b) narrow

  (c) tough   (d) wide

12. She is so <u>terrible</u> in writing.

  (a) Sad   (b) Happy

  (c) Gracious   (d) Awful

Directions (Q. Nos. 13-18) Choose the pair of synonyms from the group of words.

13. Cold, big, freezing, strong

  (a) Cold and big

  (b) Big and freezing

  (c) Cold and freezing

  (d) Big and strong

14. Powerful, destroy, ruin, happy

  (a) Powerful and happy

  (b) Destroy and ruin

  (c) Ruin and happy

  (d) Powerful and destroy

15. Clean, dirty, neat, beautiful

(a) Clean and neat
(b) Dirty and neat
(c) Clean and beautiful
(d) Dirty and beautiful

16. Tired, quiet, energetic, calm

(a) Tired and quiet
(b) Quiet and energetic
(c) Energetic and calm
(d) Quiet and calm

17. Huge, big, simple, fancy

(a) Huge and big
(b) Big and simple
(c) Simple and fancy
(d) Huge and fancy

18. Sufficient, less, enough, decline

(a) Sufficient and decline
(b) Less and enough
(c) Sufficient and enough
(d) Less and decline

Directions (Q. Nos. 19-24) Choose the correct synonyms of the underlined words to fill in the blanks.

19. That truck with the <u>noisy</u> engine is very ....

(a) quiet   (b) loud
(c) noise   (d) shout

20. My uncle is the most .... and <u>humorous</u> person in the family.

(a) comic   (b) angry
(c) generous   (d) funny

21. He was a <u>diligent</u> and .... boy who worked to achieve his goals.

(a) simple   (b) lazy
(c) hardworking   (d) soft-hearted

22. Please do not .... while I am <u>speaking</u>.

(a) talk   (b) say
(c) listen   (d) told

23. It made me <u>sad</u> to see my friend ....

(a) angry   (b) happy
(c) unhappy   (d) crying

24. If the answer is <u>false</u>, it is ....

(a) True   (b) Untrue
(c) Incorrect   (d) Right

Directions (Q. Nos. 25 and 26) Match the words given in list I with their synonyms given in list II.

25.

	List I		List II
A.	Angry	1.	Unusual
B.	Goal	2.	Tour
C.	Different	3.	Short-tempered
D.	Trip	4.	Target

Codes

	A	B	C	D		A	B	C	D
(a)	1	3	2	4	(b)	4	1	3	2
(c)	3	4	1	2	(d)	2	1	4	3

26.

	List I		List II
A.	Evil	1.	Sofa
B.	Couch	2.	Bad
C.	Great	3.	Extraordinary
D.	Ill	4.	Sick

Codes

	A	B	C	D
(a)	2	1	4	3
(b)	2	1	3	4
(c)	3	4	1	2
(d)	1	2	3	4

27. How many synonyms of 'sorrow' can you find in the box?

> Happy, content, dejection, sadness, melody, unhappiness, misery, clear, cheerful, gloom.

(a) Happy, dejection, gloom, misery
(b) Dejection, sadness, unhappiness, misery, gloom
(c) Gloom, content, melody, cheerful
(d) Content, dejection, sadness, melody

28. How many synonyms can you find for the word 'important' in the given box?

> Main, lazy, salient, unhappy, content, low, foremost, fair, kind, crucial, dark, vital, relevant, glowing, bright, essential, significant, unkind, valuable

(a) 10 (b) 12
(c) 8 (d) 6

29. Read the passage and choose the synonyms of the underlined words.

India is a democratic country. Here, people belonging to <u>different</u> religions- Hindu, Muslim, Sikh and Christians live in <u>harmony</u> with each other. India is <u>admired</u> across the world for its <u>rich</u> culture and traditions. It is the seventh-largest country in the world.

(a) Dissimilar, peace, praise, poor
(b) Uncommon, agreement, applaud, cheap
(c) Contrasting, peace, praise, affluent
(d) Unalike, brotherhood, commend, poor

Directions (Q. Nos. 30-35) Choose the synonyms for the given pictures.

30.

(a) Old
(b) New
(c) Modern
(d) Young

31.

(a) Poor (b) Wealthy
(c) Money (d) Neat

32.

(a) Weak (b) Destroy
(c) Powerful (d) Arm

33.

(a) Cold (b) Hot
(c) Jolly (d) Shy

34.

(a) Unhappy (b) Clown
(c) Satisfied (d) Crying

35.

(a) Joker (b) Happy
(c) Funny (d) Silly

Antonyms

Directions (Q. Nos. 1-5) Find the antonym of the given words. Choose the correct answer from the given options.

1. Mean
   (a) Happy   (b) Tall
   (c) Weird   (d) Nice

2. Misplace
   (a) Ignore   (b) Find
   (c) Question   (d) Loud

3. Overlook
   (a) Notice   (b) Lose
   (c) Upset   (d) Ignore

4. Noisy
   (a) Find   (b) Little
   (c) Loud   (d) Quiet

5. Excited
   (a) Calm   (b) Lose
   (c) Upset   (d) Quiet

Directions (Q. Nos. 6-10) Choose the antonym for the underlined words.

6. The soldier was very clever and <u>brave</u>.
   (a) bright   (b) fat
   (c) smart   (d) coward

7. The teacher asked us to stay away from <u>dangerous</u> places.
   (a) hazardous   (b) risky
   (c) safe   (d) plenty

8. My father is the <u>eldest</u> son of his family.
   (a) oldest   (b) stubborn
   (c) youngest   (d) polite

9. Richa did not <u>accept</u> my invitation.
   (a) rude   (b) agree
   (c) receive   (d) reject

10. It started raining as soon as I <u>entered</u> the school.
    (a) came   (b) exited
    (c) celebrated   (d) joined

Directions (Q. Nos. 11-15) Choose the correct pair of antonyms from the group of words.

11. Absent, scarce, simple, present
    (a) Absent and present
    (b) Absent and scarce
    (c) Scarce and simple
    (d) Simple and present

12. Good, nice, before, after
    (a) Good and after
    (b) Nice and before
    (c) Before and after
    (d) Nice and after

13. Clumsy, careful, filthy, careless
    (a) Clumsy and filthy
    (b) Careful and careless
    (c) Careful and filthy
    (d) Clumsy and careless

14. Encourage, kind, easy, discourage

   (a) encourage and kind

   (b) kind and easy

   (c) easy and discourage

   (d) encourage and discourage

15. Go, gentle, rough, happy

   (a) Go and happy

   (b) Gentle and rough

   (c) Gentle and happy

   (d) Rough and happy

Directions (Q. Nos. 16-21) Choose the correct antonyms of the underlined words to fill in the blanks.

16. Mary is .... in height but her sister Clera is <u>tall</u>.

   (a) small   (b) little

   (c) short   (d) high

17. He will <u>go</u> unless you .... him.

   (a) stop   (b) went

   (c) come   (d) exit

18. Although they belong to two .... families, their upbringing is <u>same</u>.

   (a) similar

   (b) alternating

   (c) happy

   (d) different

19. She always says <u>yes</u> to everyone. She should learn to say ....

   (a) conform   (b) agreement

   (c) no   (d) never

20. My .... coffee is way better than your <u>hot</u> chocolate milk.

   (a) frozen   (b) cold

   (c) freeze   (d) chilly

21. The <u>lost</u> puppy was .... in a box behind the tree.

   (a) missing   (b) lose

   (c) absent   (d) found

22. Match the words given in list I with their antonyms given in list II.

	List I		List II
A.	Angry	1.	Beautiful
B.	Ugly	2.	Calm
C.	Strong	3.	Wise
D.	Foolish	4.	Weak

Codes

	A	B	C	D
(a)	1	3	2	4
(b)	4	1	3	2
(c)	3	4	1	2
(d)	2	1	4	3

23. How many pairs of antonyms can you find in the given box.

> Fade, succeed, kind, bright, enemy, honest, legal, quiet, fail, cruel, friend, unfair, dishonest

   (a) 8   (b) 10

   (c) 5   (d) 3

24. How many antonyms can you find for the word 'rare' in the given box?

> Common, impossible, real, poor, push, usual, opposite, complex, ordinary, unsafe, habitual, scatter, familiar, regular, strict, stop, frequent, tall, sweet, fold, general

   (a) 12   (b) 6

   (c) 16   (d) 8

Directions (Q. Nos. 25-30) Choose the correct antonyms for the bold and numbered words to fix the story.

Shalini woke up with a **(25) sad** face. Today was a very **(26) ordinary** day. She was going to get a new dog from the **(27) outsider** animal shelter. Shalini jumped out of the bed and ran **(28) upstairs**. Her mom and dad were sitting at the breakfast table eating breakfast. "Get ready **(29) slow**. We need to leave the house by 9:00 am.", mom said. "I can't wait", Shalini said happily. She ate her breakfast, brushed her teeth and got dressed. Shalini wondered, "What should I call my **(30) old** puppy?"

25. (a) calm   (b) happy
    (c) cute   (d) irritated

26. (a) special   (b) simple
    (c) unimportant   (d) regular

27. (a) global   (b) national
    (c) local   (d) neighbourhood

28. (a) sidestairs   (b) under
    (c) down   (d) downstairs

29. (a) fast   (b) quick
    (c) hurry   (d) faster

30. (a) modern   (b) ancient
    (c) new   (d) fashionable

Directions (Q. Nos. 31-35) Choose the antonyms for the given pictures.

31.

(a) Girl   (b) Boy
(c) Female   (d) Lady

32.

(a) Tough   (b) Solid
(c) Soft   (d) Pure

33.

(a) Thin   (b) Thick
(c) Adult   (d) Young

34.

(a) Bed   (b) Awake
(c) Wake   (d) Asleep

35.

(a) Child
(b) Baby
(c) Happy
(d) Old

Chapter 15

Word Pair and Odd One Out

Directions (Q. Nos. 1-7) Complete the word analogy by choosing the correct option.

1. Fire : Hot : : Snow : ?
   (a) Frozen   (b) Yellow
   (c) Warm   (d) Tasty

2. Spend : Save : : Give : ?
   (a) Watch   (b) Receive
   (c) Say   (d) Ask

3. Brush : Paint : : Pen : ?
   (a) Eat   (b) Steal
   (c) Write   (d) Have

4. Race : Competition : : Party : ?
   (a) Career   (b) Preparation
   (c) Game   (d) Celebration

5. Mother : Female : : Father : ?
   (a) Angry   (b) Kind
   (c) Male   (d) Thin

6. Wall : Room : : ?
   (a) Lettuce : Coffee
   (b) Dog : Cat
   (c) Wheel : Car
   (d) Song : Dance

7. Seatbelt : Car :: Helmet : ?
   (a) Cycle   (b) Bike   (c) Truck   (d) Jeep

Directions (Q. Nos. 8-14) Complete the word analogy by choosing the correct homophones.

8. Heel : Heal :: Tale : ?
   (a) Tell   (b) Tail   (c) Tall   (d) Trail

9. Weak : : Week :: Waist : ?
   (a) Wait   (b) Waits
   (c) Waste   (d) Waists

10. Hole : Whole :: Mail : ?
    (a) Mell   (b) Mall   (c) Melt   (d) Male

11. Know : No :: One : ?
    (a) Once   (b) Won   (c) Win   (d) Wons

12. I : Eye :: Die : ?
    (a) Dye   (b) Died
    (c) Dying   (d) Dry

13. To : Two :: Steel : ?
    (a) Stale   (b) Stail
    (c) Stole   (d) Steal

14. Meet : Meat :: Deer : ?
    (a) Dare   (b) Draw
    (c) Dear   (d) Dire

Directions (Q. Nos. 15-22) Complete the word analogy by choosing the correct homonyms.

15. Bear : to cope with something :: bear : ?
    (a) a drink   (b) a large animal
    (c) a soft toy   (d) None of these

16. Band : a musical group :: band : ?
    (a) a ring
    (b) a band-aid
    (c) a musical instrument
    (d) a person

17. Kind : type :: kind : ?
    (a) rude   (b) arrogant
    (c) short-tempered   (d) caring

18. Mean : not nice :: mean : ?
    (a) centre   (b) best
    (c) average   (d) None of these

19. Lie : to tell a falsehood :: lie : ?
    (a) to sleep   (b) to recline
    (c) to sit   (d) to stand

20. Pound : to beat :: pound : ?
    (a) unit of distance (b) unit of currency
    (c) unit of length   (d) unit of weight

21. Spring : a coiled metal :: spring : ?
    (a) to jump   (b) to flow
    (c) a season   (d) a weather

22. Light : pale in color :: light : ?
    (a) to set on fire   (b) to put out fire
    (c) lighter   (d) None of these

Directions (Q. Nos. 23-40) Find the odd one out.

23. (a) book   (b) pen   (c) toy   (d) Herd

24. (a) anger   (b) hunger
    (c) shock   (d) achievable

25. (a) happy   (b) sad
    (c) running   (d) angry

26. (a) sparrow   (b) jury
    (c) committee   (d) troop

27. (a) steel   (b) iron
    (c) gang   (d) rubber

28. (a) radio   (b) camera
    (c) computer   (d) microsoft

29. (a) sleeping   (b) joyfully
    (c) walks   (d) talked

30. (a) evil   (b) bad
    (c) tidy   (d) wicked

31. (a) Victoria   (b) Amazon
    (c) India   (d) Nation

32. (a) happily   (b) slow
    (c) equally   (d) quickly

33. (a) Taj Mahal   (b) We
    (c) She   (d) He

34. (a) cold   (b) frozen
    (c) refrigerator   (d) chilly

35. (a) hate   (b) beautiful
    (c) love   (d) honesty

36. (a) often   (b) of
    (c) in   (d) at

37. (a) clear   (b) big
    (c) smooth   (d) clearly

38. (a) talked   (b) eats
    (c) walked   (d) told

39. (a) blank   (b) tight
    (c) empty   (d) hollow

40. (a) cleverer   (b) fastest
    (c) slower   (d) simpler

Spelling Test

Directions (Q. Nos. 1-12) Find the correctly spelt word.

1. (a) Carefull   (b) Cerefull
   (c) Careful   (d) Cereful

2. (a) Paket   (b) Packet
   (c) Paccet   (d) Pakket

3. (a) Refrigerator   (b) Refrigrator
   (c) Rafrigrater   (d) Refregerater

4. (a) Quien   (b) Quin
   (c) Quine   (d) Queen

5. (a) Fethers   (b) Fethars
   (c) Feathers   (d) Feathars

6. (a) Yoghurt   (b) Yougurt
   (c) Yogart   (d) Yoghart

7. (a) Sliping   (b) Sleaping
   (c) Sleeping   (d) Sleepping

8. (a) Stakk   (b) Stacc
   (c) Staac   (d) Stack

9. (a) Advencher   (b) Adventure
   (c) Advanture   (d) Advenchure

10. (a) Twelfth   (b) Twelth
    (c) Twelveth   (d) Twelvth

11. (a) Miserable
    (b) Mizrable
    (c) Misrable
    (d) Misarable

12. (a) Tripple   (b) Triple
    (c) Trepple   (d) Trypal

Directions (Q. Nos. 13-25) Fill in the blanks with correctly spelt words.

13. One who flies a plane is called a ....
    (a) pilet   (b) pilot
    (c) pilat   (d) paillot

14. The child was eating a ....
    (a) toffee   (b) tofee
    (c) toofee   (d) toffe

15. Children should stay away from the ....
    (a) flemes   (b) fleems
    (c) phlames   (d) flames

16. The teacher asked Rohini to read a ....
    (a) paragraf   (b) paregraph
    (c) paragraph   (d) pergraf

17. Raman was .... a bicycle.
    (a) riding   (b) ridding
    (c) riddeng   (d) ridiing

18. These bushes grow to .... of up to five feet.
    (a) heihgts
    (b) hieghts
    (c) heights
    (d) heigts

19. She used to read .... everyday.
   (a) newspapaer
   (b) newspaper
   (c) newpaper
   (d) neewspaperr

20. I am going for shopping with my ....
   (a) pairents   (b) parants
   (c) perents   (d) parents

21. The children were .... with laughter.
   (a) screaming   (b) screeming
   (c) scrieming   (d) scriming

22. Tie the two ropes .... with a secure knot.
   (a) togather   (b) twogather
   (c) together   (d) towgather

23. Do you .... in magic?
   (a) believe   (b) beleive
   (c) beleeve   (d) beleave

24. Can you help me spell .... ?
   (a) rinoceros   (b) rinoseros
   (c) rynoceros   (d) rhinoceros

25. I often come to this ....
   (a) restorant   (b) restaurant
   (c) restorent   (d) restaurent

Directions (Q. Nos. 26-35) Find the word with incorrect spelling.

26. (a) Yesterday   (b) Distance
   (c) Ziper   (d) Citizen

27. (a) Crow   (b) Parrot
   (c) Eegle   (d) Hawk

28. (a) Loyel   (b) Voyage
   (c) Joyful   (d) Journey

29. (a) Globe   (b) Company
   (c) Security   (d) Profeet

30. (a) Radio   (b) Vaccum
   (c) Computer   (d) Television

31. (a) Basket   (b) Breakfast
   (c) Cariies   (d) Caught

32. (a) Crawl   (b) Crazy
   (c) Dollar   (d) Boxis

33. (a) Cried   (b) Emosions
   (c) Happen   (d) Guess

34. (a) Fourgot   (b) Knew
   (c) Laugh   (d) Kettle

35. (a) Shelf
   (b) Straight
   (c) Wrong
   (d) Trubble

Idioms and Phrases

Directions (Q. Nos. 1-10) Choose the correct meaning of the given idioms.

1. Cost an arm and a leg
   (a) cost of an arm   (b) very expensive
   (c) cost of a leg   (d) very long

2. Once in a blue moon
   (a) rarely
   (b) when blue moon occurs
   (c) feeling sad
   (d) occurring only once

3. To feel under the weather
   (a) to bend down
   (b) to feel according to weather
   (c) to feel low or ill
   (d) to sleep

4. Put someone down
   (a) to put down
   (b) to criticise someone
   (c) to send away
   (d) to praise someone

5. Sum and substance
   (a) summary of something
   (b) to add things
   (c) irrelevant part of something
   (d) to subtract and then add

6. Black and blue
   (a) badly bruised
   (b) to turn black
   (c) to turn blue
   (d) to be in pain

7. Spins a yarn
   (a) to tease or mock one with bad-mannered or unpleasant names.
   (b) to create ideas that are impractical, unlikely and impossible.
   (c) to tell a long and far-fetched story.
   (d) to spoil somebody's chance of doing something.

8. A bolt from the blue
   (a) lightening
   (b) to be angry
   (c) a complete surprise
   (d) bolt in blue colour

9. To bell the cat
   (a) tie a bell on cat   (b) to slow down
   (c) a very easy task   (d) to face the risk

10. Hard and fast
    (a) strict
    (b) cause of trouble
    (c) facing the risk
    (d) serious

Directions (Q. Nos. 11-15) Choose the correct idioms and phrases for the given meanings.

11. Something which causes a quarrel
    (a) a bed of roses
    (b) apple of accord
    (c) a bone of contention
    (d) a bosom friend

12. False tears

(a) crocodile tears   (b) hyena tears
(c) bread and butter (d) a herculean task

13. A literary man

(a) a man of articles (b) a man of letters
(c) a bosom friend   (d) a black sheep

14. Too nervous to do something

(a) in the doghouse
(b) black and blue
(c) to get cold feet
(d) to beat around the bush

15. To give false alarm

(a) to listen eagerly
(b) to turn pale
(c) to keep off starvation
(d) to cry wolf

Directions (Q. Nos. 16-22) Identify the idioms and phrases in the given sentences.

16. If you want to be a singer, you should give it a shot.

(a) a singer   (b) give it
(c) a shot   (d) give it a shot

17. He drops in off and on for a chat with me.

(a) drops in   (b) off and on
(c) on for a chat   (d) chat with me

18. I have to settle an account with him.

(a) have to settle
(b) account with
(c) settle an account
(d) None of the above

19. The teacher asked us to talk about the pros and cons of industrial development.

(a) talk about
(b) cons of industrial development
(c) pros of industrial development
(d) pros and cons

20. It's late; let's call it a day.

(a) call it a day   (b) late
(c) it's late   (d) lets call

21. I saw Sunita at the store, and she gave me the cold shoulder.

(a) at the store
(b) gave me
(c) cold shoulder
(d) gave me the cold

22. If you think that doing this Maths problem is a piece of cake, just try it.

(a) try it
(b) a piece of cake
(c) you think
(d) problem is a piece of cake

Directions (Q. Nos. 23-25) Fill in the blanks with correct idioms or phrases.

23. Once .... some monkeys can be seen in this area.

(a) in a blue moon   (b) in a moon
(c) in a red moon   (d) None of these

24. The student was beating .... when he was asked to answer the question.

(a) around the drum
(b) around the grass
(c) around the bush
(d) around the tree

25. He realised that there was no use of crying ....

(a) flown water
(b) spilt water
(c) thrown away milk
(d) over spilt milk

Chapter 18

One Word Substitution

Directions (Q. Nos. 1-20) Select the one word which substitutes the given sentence.

1. A person who looks after sick patients.
   - (a) Lawyer
   - (b) Teacher
   - (c) Doctor
   - (d) Writer

2. A person who mends shoes.
   - (a) Jeweller
   - (b) Helper
   - (c) Plumber
   - (d) Cobbler

3. A person who sells medicines.
   - (a) Plumber
   - (b) Guard
   - (c) Teacher
   - (d) Chemist

4. A person who cannot read and write.
   - (a) Electrician
   - (b) Illiterate
   - (c) Literate
   - (d) Milkman

5. A person who makes clothes.
   - (a) Tailor
   - (b) Carpenter
   - (c) Cobbler
   - (d) Writer

6. A place where criminals are kept.
   - (a) School
   - (b) Zoo
   - (c) Prison
   - (d) Society

7. A person who paints walls and houses.
   - (a) Helper
   - (b) Painter
   - (c) Driver
   - (d) Electrician

8. A place where you go to worship.
   - (a) School
   - (b) Market
   - (c) Temple
   - (d) Office

9. A place where you go to exercise.
   - (a) Parlour
   - (b) Gym
   - (c) Mall
   - (d) Tution

10. A place where you go out to eat.
    - (a) Restaurant
    - (b) Church
    - (c) Garden
    - (d) Hospital

11. A person who manages books in the library.
    - (a) Teacher
    - (b) Librarian
    - (c) Dancer
    - (d) Receptionist

12. A person who cooks food in a restaurant.
    - (a) Chef
    - (b) Waiter
    - (c) Painter
    - (d) Singer

13. A person who cuts hair.
    - (a) Cobbler
    - (b) Plumber
    - (c) Tailor
    - (d) Barber

14. A person who flies aeroplanes.
    - (a) Pilot
    - (b) Astronaut
    - (c) Engineer
    - (d) Astronomer

15. A person who cures your toothache.
    - (a) Physiotherapist
    - (b) Counsellor
    - (c) Dentist
    - (d) Mechanic

16. A person who manages work.
    - (a) Nurse
    - (b) Manager
    - (c) Mason
    - (d) Guard

17. A person who repairs pipes and leakages.
    - (a) Plumber
    - (b) Carpenter
    - (c) Magician
    - (d) Chemist

18. A person who acts in movies and serials.
    - (a) Musician
    - (b) Director
    - (c) Singer
    - (d) Actor

19. A person who makes furniture.
    - (a) Carpenter
    - (b) Artist
    - (c) Designer
    - (d) Leader

20. A person who writes books.
    - (a) Driver
    - (b) Author
    - (c) Printer
    - (d) Doctor

Directions (Q. Nos. 21-25) Choose the correct explanation of the given one word.

21. Indelible
    - (a) Excessively concerned with minor details or rules
    - (b) Making marks that cannot be removed
    - (c) Certain to happen
    - (d) Incapable of making mistakes or being wrong

22. Potable
    - (a) Easy to carry from one place to another
    - (b) In exactly the same words as were used originally
    - (c) Safe to drink
    - (d) A self-governing country

23. Orchard
    - (a) A piece of enclosed land planted with fruit trees
    - (b) A place where bodies are kept for identification
    - (c) A room or building for sick children in a boarding school
    - (d) A place where wild animal live

24. Constellation
    - (a) A group of worshippers
    - (b) A small fleet of ships or boats
    - (c) A large group of people
    - (d) A series of stars

25. Egotist
    - (a) One who believes in fate
    - (b) One who often talks of his achievements
    - (c) One who is hard to please
    - (d) A lover of good food

Chapter 19

Reading Comprehension

Passage 1

Directions (Q. Nos. 1-5) Given below is a paragraph. Read it and answer the questions that follow from the options given below.

Jeddi and his Kangaroo

Long ago, in a desert outside the city, lived Jeddi, a young boy.

Jeddi and his father were out hunting one day when they saw a baby Kangaroo lying on the ground.

Jeddi said, 'It's hurt Dad.'

'Yes it is,' said Jeddi's father, 'Shall we help it?'

'Yes,' said Jeddi.

Jeddi and his father took the Kangaroo back to their camp in the desert.

Each day they gave the Kangaroo some food to eat and some water to drink. After about three weeks the Kangaroo was well again.

Jeddi said to the Kangaroo, "Now you are better...you are free to hop away and go back to the other Kangaroos."

Do you think the Kangaroo hopped away? No, it stayed with Jeddi and became his pet.

1. Jeddi lived with his father ....
   (a) in a big city
   (b) far away in the desert
   (c) in a huge house
   (d) near the sea-shore

2. What did Jeddi and his father find out while hunting one day?
   (a) A bag full of money.
   (b) A trapped lion.
   (c) A small Kangaroo lying hurt.
   (d) A small bird bleeding.

3. Why do you think the Kangaroo stayed with Jeddi?
   (a) Kangaroo liked deserts.
   (b) Other animals became his friends.
   (c) Jeddi and Kangaroo became good friends.
   (d) Kangaroo was no more.

4. An antonym of the word 'young' can be ....
   (a) new   (b) away   (c) old   (d) better

5. A synonym of the word 'hurt' can be ....
   (a) hopped   (b) hoped
   (c) injured   (d) heated

Passage 2

Directions (Q. Nos. 6-10) Read the passage and answer the questions that follow. Choose the correct answer from the options given below.

Once upon a time there was a hungry fox. One night he was searching for some food. He met a little kitten and was tempted to eat her. When he tried to pounce on the kitten, the kitten said, "Oh, don't eat me. I know where the farmer keeps his cheese. Come with me and see."

The kitten lead him into the farmyard, where there was a deep well. "Now, look in here and you will see the cheese," she said.

The fox looked down the well and saw the moon reflected in the water. He thought it was a cheese ball. The foolish fox jumped into the well and was drowned.

6. How did the fox feel when he saw the kitten?
   (a) He thought of making the kitten his friend.
   (b) He was tempted to eat the kitten.
   (c) He thought of playing with the kitten.
   (d) He wanted to kill the kitten.

7. Where did the kitten take the fox?
   (a) To the forest   (b) To her home
   (c) To the farmyard (d) To the Lion king

8. What did the fox find in the well?
   (a) A cheese cake
   (b) Reflection of the moon
   (c) Hot water
   (d) A bucket

9. The meaning of the word 'pounce' will be to ....
   (a) sit there   (b) jump and catch
   (c) suddenly   (d) run away

10. The antonym of the word 'foolish' will be ....
    (a) comic   (b) serious
    (c) wise   (d) strong

Passage 3

Directions (Q. Nos. 11-15) Read the passage and answer the questions that follow. Choose the correct answer from the options given below.

There are four major domains of the Earth- Lithosphere, Atmosphere, Hydrosphere and Biosphere. The solid portion of the Earth is called Lithosphere. The large land masses are known as continents. All continents lie in lithosphere. There are seven continents. Asia is the largest continent and Australia is the smallest.

The part of the Earth which is covered with water is called Hydrosphere. It includes – The Pacific Ocean, The Atlantic Ocean, The Indian Ocean, The Southern Ocean and The Arctic Ocean. The Pacific Ocean is the largest ocean.

The Earth is surrounded by a layer of gases called the Atmosphere. There are five layers in the atmosphere. The part of the Earth where all life is found is called the Biosphere.

11. In which domain of the Earth, do the continents lie?
    (a) Lithosphere   (b) Atmosphere
    (c) Hydrosphere   (d) Biosphere

12. Which part of the Earth is called Hydrosphere?
    (a) The solid part
    (b) The part where all life is found
    (c) The part that is surrounded by gases
    (d) The part that is covered with water

13. How many layers are there in the atmosphere?
    (a) Four layers   (b) Three layers
    (c) Five layers   (d) Two layers

14. Which is the largest ocean on Earth?
    (a) The Pacific Ocean
    (b) The Atlantic Ocean
    (c) The Indian Ocean
    (d) The Arctic Ocean

15. Find the odd one out from the given options.
    (a) Lithosphere   (b) Hydrosphere
    (c) Australia   (d) Biosphere

Poem 1

Directions (Q. Nos. 16-20) Read the poem and answer the questions that follow. Choose the correct answer from the options given below.

Lovely Things

Bread is a lovely thing to eat -
God bless the barley and the wheat!
A lovely thing to breathe is air -
God bless the sunshine everywhere!
The Earth's a lovely place to know -
God bless the folks that come and go!
Alive's a lovely thing to be -
Giver of life - we say - bless Thee!

HM Sarson

16. What makes bread a lovely thing to eat?
    (a) Rice
    (b) Barley
    (c) Wheat
    (d) Both (b) and (c)

17. What makes air a lovely thing to breathe?
    (a) Bread   (b) God
    (c) Sunshine   (d) All of these

18. In the poem, what is the other name used to refer to God?
    (a) Folks
    (b) Giver of life
    (c) Bless Thee
    (d) Alive

19. The meaning of the word 'folks' will be ....
    (a) people   (b) non-living things
    (c) birds   (d) plants and trees

20. The antonym of the word 'alive' will be ....
    (a) shivering   (b) burried
    (c) thinking   (d) dead

Poem 2

Directions (Q. Nos. 21-25) Read the poem and answer the questions that follow. Choose the correct answer from the options given below.

Little white lily
Sat by a stone,
    Drooping and waiting
    Till the sun shone.
Little white lily
Sunshine has fed;
    Little white lily
    Is lifting her head.
Little white lily
Droops with pain,
    Waiting and waiting
    For the wet rain.
Little white lily
Holds her cup;
    Rain is fast falling
    And filling it up.

George MacDonald

21. Where is little white lily sitting?

(a) By a wall.
(b) By a stone.
(c) In the flower pot.
(d) By a window.

22. When did little white lily lift her head?

(a) When it received sunshine.
(b) When it received air.
(c) When it woke up.
(d) When it was happy.

23. Why does little white lily hold her cup?

(a) To receive sunshine.
(b) To receive oxygen.
(c) To pass it on.
(d) To receive rainwater.

24. The antonym of the word 'wet' will be
....

(a) liquid   (b) dry
(c) moist   (d) watery

25. The synonym of the word 'shine' will be
....

(a) smooth   (b) dull
(c) sparkle   (d) creamy

Poem 3

Direction (Q. Nos. 26-30) Read the poem and answer the questions that follow. Choose the correct answer from the options given below.

The moon is a sphere, big and white
It loves to reflect the sun's bright light.
It goes on a journey every 28th day
Around the earth, a hide and seek game it
will play.
In the beginning, it is new
Out of sight from me and you
Then it waxes in white
As it grows in its right
Waxing crescent and quarter, then
gibbous too
When full, the phases are halfway
through!
Now it flips to the left and starts to wane
As it fades away in its orbit lane.
Waning gibbous and quarter then
crescent too
It's completed its orbit and back to new!

Betty Sanchez

26. What is the above poem about?

(a) Sun and its uses
(b) Moon and its different shapes
(c) Beautiful stars
(d) Space

27. According to the poem, what does the moon reflect?

(a) The bright light of the sun
(b) The light of the planets
(c) The light of the earth
(d) The light of torch

28. Name the game that the moon plays in the above poem.

(a) Duck, duck, goose
(b) Hide and seek game
(c) Musical chairs
(d) Capture the flag

29. The meaning of the word 'sphere' will be
....

(a) Angle   (b) Square
(c) Circle   (d) Cube

30. The antonym of the word 'beginning' will be ....

(a) Creation   (b) Start
(c) End   (d) Dawn

Spoken and Written Expression

Directions (Q. Nos. 1-10) Complete the following dialogues. Choose from the options given below.

1. Shopkeeper: Good morning! How may I help you?

   Child :............ .
   (a) Will want a chocolate and a toffee.
   (b) I want a chocolate and a toffee.
   (c) I do not want a chocolate and a toffee.
   (d) Yes, I wanted the two chocolate and two toffee.

2. Doctor: What has happened, son?

   Patient: ....
   (a) I falled and hurt myself.
   (b) I felled and hurt myself.
   (c) I falled and hurted myself.
   (d) I fell and hurt myself.

3. Preeti: Mummy, ... breakfast today?

   Mother: Butter toasts and milk.
   (a) What did you make for the?
   (b) What have you prepared for the
   (c) What are you making today?
   (d) What did you prepare today?

4. Rahul: Please don't hang up the phone.

   Ravi: ....
   (a) I don't want to talk to you.
   (b) Don't call me again.
   (c) I'm having another call. I will call you later.
   (d) I am hanging up the phone.

5. Harsh: Hey! I have great news. I have been selected to play for the Indian Cricket Team.

   Ben: ....
   (a) That's very bad.
   (b) Congratulations. I am so happy for you.
   (c) I am jealous of you.
   (d) I am not happy for you.

6. Teacher: Why were you absent yesterday?

   Shiv: ....
   (a) Because I did not want to come to school.
   (b) Because I had not done my homework.
   (c) Because Ajay was not coming.
   (d) Because I was not feeling well, Ma'am.

7. Customer: How much is this dress for?

Shopkeeper: ……………………………….. .

(a) It is for ₹ 1000. Would you like to try it?

(b) It is not for you.

(c) You cannot buy it. It is very expensive.

(d) I don't want to sell it. Go away!

8. Amit: Do you want to play tennis?

Rohan: ………………… .

(a) Yes, I don't want to play tennis.

(b) That's a good idea! Let's play.

(c) Not possible for I.

(d) Yes, but not with you.

9. Sneha: I want to invite you to my birthday party. Will you come?

Shreyarsh: ……………………………… .

(a) No! I don't like you.

(b) I hate birthday parties.

(c) Yes, I will come. Thank you for inviting me.

(d) No, I will sit at home and watch movies.

10. Jasmine: Do you want to help me draw?

Riya: ………………………….. .

(a) No, do it by yourself!

(b) I hate drawing.

(c) We are not kids anymore.

(d) Yes, I would love to help you.

Directions (Q. Nos. 11-13) Complete the following dialogues. Choose from the options given below.

11.

(a) like to have?   (b) liked to had?

(c) liked?   (d) likes?

12.

(a) we will decorating the classroom.

(b) we will decorate it.

(c) we will be decorate the classroom.

(d) we will decorated the it.

13.

(a) gone out?   (b) going out?

(c) go out?   (d) went out?

Directions (Q. Nos. 14-16) See the picture carefully and fill in the blanks.

14. ……….. is knitting a sweater.

(a) The cat   (b) The children

(c) The dog   (d) The grandmother

15. The little girl is reading …………. favourite book.

(a) his   (b) its

(c) her   (d) their

16. The dog is sitting .... the ground.

    (a) under

    (b) on

    (c) around

    (d) between

Directions (Q. Nos. 17 and 18) See the picture carefully and fill in the blanks.

17. There are .... children in the room.

    (a) two

    (b) three

    (c) four

    (d) five

18. The children .... books.

    (a) is reading

    (b) was reading

    (c) are reading

    (d) am reading

Directions (Q. Nos. 19 and 20) Choose the sentences that match the pictures.

19.

    (a) The children are exercising.

    (b) The children are playing.

    (c) The children are lying on the floor.

    (d) The children are jumping.

20.

    (a) A teacher is writing in the class.

    (b) A teacher is laughing in the class.

    (c) A teacher is sitting in the class.

    (d) A teacher is teaching in the class.

PRACTICE SET 

1. Match the following subjects with their predicates.

	Subject		Predicate
A.	A Doctor	1.	went to a party.
B.	I	2.	pet is missing.
C.	My	3.	invented the bulb.
D.	Edison	4.	treats patients.

Codes

	A	B	C	D		A	B	C	D
(a)	4	1	3	2	(b)	2	1	4	3
(c)	4	1	2	3	(d)	1	2	3	4

2. Identify the common noun in the sentence.

A bird came inside my room.

(a) came (b) inside (c) my (d) bird

3. Fill in the blank with a suitable pronoun.

God helps ...... who help themselves.

(a) these (b) such (c) those (d) that

4. Find the verb(s) in the following sentence.

The birds kept on singing, cuddling and kissing.

(a) singing (b) cuddling
(c) kissing (d) All of these

5. Fill in the correct verb to form the sentence in past continuous tense.

I ...... a cricket match last night.

(a) watched (b) was watching
(c) were watching (d) watching

6. Choose the sentence with the correct use of articles.

(a) An ant and a grasshopper became friends.

(b) A ant and an grasshopper became friends.

(c) A ant came to meet an grasshopper.

(d) An ant came to meet an grasshopper.

7. Fill in the blank with a suitable adjective of quantity.

You can take ...... cookies from the plate.

(a) any (b) much (c) most (d) some

8. Identify the adverb in the sentence.

The quick, brown fox jumped lazily over the dog.

(a) lazily (b) quick (c) brown (d) on

9. Complete the sentence using appropriate conjunction.

Make hay .... the Sun shines.

(a) and (b) while (c) but (d) or

10. Identify the preposition(s) in the sentence.

I kept the book on the table but somebody kept it under it.

(a) on (b) under
(c) on, under (d) but

11. Find the correctly punctuated sentence from the following.

(a) Kamal went to a Party Today.

(b) Shahid and Mira got married last year.

(c) Wow! What a great catch!

(d) I like to eat chocolates,

12. Rearrange the following letters to make a meaningful word.

OLBIEM

(a) MOLIBE   (b) MELOBI

(c) MEOLIB   (d) MOBILE

13. Rearrange the following words to make a meaningful sentence.

dog's/Nandu/is/pet/name/my

(a) My dog's pet is name Nandu.

(b) My dog's name pet is Nandu.

(c) My name pet dog's is Nandu.

(d) My pet dog's name is Nandu.

14. What is the antonym of the underlined word in the sentence?

He went to a <u>noisy</u> park.

(a) quiet   (b) quite

(c) quick   (d) naughty

15. Choose a word for the right side that best expresses a relation similar to that of the pair on the left side.

Ball : Play : : Pen : ....

(a) White   (b) Write   (c) Study   (d) Read

16. Fill in the blank using an appropriate collective noun.

A .... of bees was hovering over the flowers.

(a) herd   (b) flock

(c) swarm   (d) army

17. The abstract noun of 'brave' is

(a) braveness   (b) bravity

(c) brevity   (d) bravery

18. Fill in the blank using the correct form of adjective.

Honey is .... than sugar.

(a) sweet   (b) sweetest

(c) sweeter   (d) more sweet

19. Choose a suitable preposition to fill the blank.

The train went .... the tunnel.

(a) in   (b) across

(c) between   (d) through

20. Fill in the blank using articles.

.... Octopus is .... aquatic animal.

(a) An, the   (b) The, a

(c) The, an   (d) A, a

Directions (Q. Nos. 21-25) Read the passage and answer the questions given below.

Teepu had a bad day. He was punished by his class teacher as he had not completed his homework. The teacher asked him to go out of the class. She also wrote a note in his diary which he had to get signed from his parents. When Teepu reached home from school, he was scared to show the note to his parents. He did not know what to do. If he did not get it signed, he would not be allowed to attend the class tomorrow. He planned to sign the note himself.

21. Why was Teepu punished?

(a) Because he completed his homework.

(b) Because he came late to class.

(c) Because he did not complete his homework.

(d) Because he did not complete his classwork.

22. What did Teepu's teacher do?

(a) She wrote a note in Teepu's diary.

(b) She punished Teepu.

(c) She took the class to a picnic.

(d) Both (a) and (b)

23. Who had to sign the note in Teepu's diary?

(a) Teepu's father
(b) Teepu's parents
(c) Teepu's brother
(d) Teepu's grandparents

24. The antonym of 'punished' is

(a) praised   (b) scolded
(c) scored   (d) befriended

25. "He planned to sign the note himself."
In the above sentence, 'he' stands for

(a) Teepu's father
(b) Teepu's class teacher
(c) Teepu's brother
(d) Teepu

26. Choose the synonym of the given word.
Valiant

(a) Nervous   (b) Cowardly
(c) Brave   (d) Quick

27. Find the odd one out.

(a) Water   (b) Bottle   (c) Shop   (d) Pencil

28. Fill in the blank with correctly spelt word.
He was riding a .... without helmet.

(a) Motarcicle   (b) Motorcaical
(c) Motorcycle   (d) Moterciacle

29. Choose the word with incorrect spelling.

(a) Listen   (b) Option
(c) Speaking   (d) Hamer

30. Choose the correct meaning of the underlined idiom.
In the end he had to eat the humble pie.

(a) make a humble apology
(b) getting angry
(c) eating a pie
(d) None of the above

31. Choose the correct idiom for the given meaning.
To scold someone

(a) To put someone down
(b) A piece of cake
(c) To take to task
(d) Gift of the gab

32. Choose the one word for the given words.
A number of sailors working on a ship

(a) Flock   (b) Fleet
(c) Pirates   (d) Crew

33. Choose the correct option.
Antiseptic

(a) A medicine to counteract poison
(b) A substance that destroys germs
(c) Free from infection
(d) A cure for all diseases

Directions (Q. Nos. 34 and 35) Complete the following dialogues.

34. Mother : Thank God for Sundays!
Daughter : Mummy, today ....

(a) I can help you with the cleaning of the house.
(b) I can help you by the cleaning of the house.
(c) I can't help you for the cleaning of the house.
(d) I can helped you with a cleaning of the house?

35. Ravi : .... Dad.
Father : Yes, it feels good.

(a) Bad to have you back early today
(b) Good to had you early today
(c) Good to have you back early today
(d) Good in having your back early today

PRACTICE SET 

1. What is the abstract noun of 'Modest'?
   (a) Modern   (b) Mode
   (c) Model   (d) Modesty

2. Match the following.

List I (Subject)	List II (Predicate)
A. It	1. clothes are missing.
B. She	2. are coming now.
C. They	3. is going to school.
D. Their	4. rained yesterday.

Codes

	A	B	C	D		A	B	C	D
(a)	1	2	3	4	(b)	4	2	3	1
(c)	4	3	2	1	(d)	3	4	1	2

3. Fill in the blank with a suitable adjective.
   The student fell down. His school bag was very ....
   (a) light   (b) small
   (c) heavy   (d) strong

4. Identify the sentence in which articles are used properly.
   (a) A monkey went to an hotel.
   (b) A apples are good for everyone.
   (c) An almirah was shifted from this room.
   (d) A honest man is praised by all.

5. Choose the correct sentence.
   (a) We can buy a t-shirt if we buy a coat for Rahul.
   (b) We can either buy a t-shirt or a coat for Rahul.
   (c) We can buy a t-shirt because we buy a coat for Rahul.
   (d) We can buy a t-shirt yet we buy a coat for Rahul.

6. Which sentence is punctuated properly?
   (a) Navin, Pravin and Shirin are playing Golf,
   (b) Navin, Pravin and Shirin are playing golf.
   (c) Navin, Pravin and shirin are playing Golf.
   (d) Navin Pravin and Shirin are playing golf.

7. Frame a meaningful word from the given letters.
   NIBLDUIG
   (a) Budding   (b) Building
   (c) Digging   (d) Double

8. Find the odd-one out.
   (a) Cold drink   (b) Cold coffee
   (c) Soup   (d) Lemonade

9. The antonym of the underlined word in the sentence is
   We should prevent <u>cruelty</u> against animals.
   (a) kind   (b) kindly
   (c) reality   (d) kindness

10. Choose the correct helping verb to fill in the blank.
   Tendulkar could play cricket when he .... three.
   (a) is   (b) was
   (c) are   (d) an

Directions (Q. Nos. 11 and 12) Complete the following dialogues.

11. Teacher : Rita, the function begins at 6 pm. You are going to welcome the guests.

Rita   : I'll do that Ma'am. ....

(a) What do I having to say?
(b) What do I had to say?
(c) What did I have to say?
(d) What do I have to say?

12. Ramesh: Ratan, your leg is in plaster! ....

Ratan   : I was hit by a speeding three-wheeler.

(a) What will happened?
(b) What did happened?
(c) What happened?
(d) What was happened?

13. Choose the correct one word for the phrase given below.
A place where orphans are housed.

(a) House   (b) Night shelter
(c) Orphanage   (d) Garage

14. Choose the correct phrase for the given one word.
Astrology

(a) The study of stars
(b) The study of birds
(c) The study of trees
(d) The study of humans

15. Choose the pronoun for the underlined noun in the given sentence.
Mr. Sharma is <u>Arun's</u> father.

(a) He   (b) His   (c) Him   (d) Her

16. Complete the word analogy.
Keyboard : Computer :: Toes :?

(a) Hands (b) Fingers (c) Legs   (d) Feet

17. Change the given sentence into simple present tense.
My wife will bake a cake.

(a) My wife is bakes a cake.
(b) My wife bakes a cake.
(c) My wife baked a cake.
(d) My wife is backed a cake.

Directions (Q. Nos. 18-21) Fill in the blanks.

18. My mother was sleeping so I went into her room very ....

(a) hastily (b) lazily (c) swiftly (d) quietly

19. The rivers lies .... the two mountains.

(a) through   (b) above
(c) inside   (d) between

20. Are the questions right .... wrong?

(a) but   (b) or   (c) and   (d) while

21. Sanya .... clothes to help her mother.

(a) is washing   (b) washing
(c) will washing   (d) will washed

22. Rearrange the following words to form a meaningful sentence.
Make/noise/the students/lot of/a/in/the /class.

(a) A students make the lot of noise in the class.
(b) The students make the lot of noise in a class.
(c) The students make a lot of noise in the class.
(d) The class students in the make a lot of noise.

23. Choose the correct spelling.

(a) Priserve   (b) Preverse
(c) Prezerve   (d) Preserve

24. Find the word with incorrect spelling.
 (a) Enviroment   (b) Triumph
 (c) Plaster   (d) Development

25. The word that can be a synonym for the words 'faucet' and 'strike'
 (a) Blow   (b) Drop   (c) Tap   (d) Hand

26. Choose the correct meaning of the given idiom.
 A black sheep
 (a) An unworthy person in a family or a group
 (b) A dark shiny object
 (c) A costly item
 (d) A funny man

27. Identify the idiom in the given sentence. I wish you would not put your nose in other people's matters.
 (a) Your nose in   (b) Put your nose in
 (c) In where it   (d) Not wanted

28. Fill in the blanks with appropriate articles.
 I saw .... accident of .... car.
 (a) a, a   (b) the, an   (c) an, a   (d) an, an

29. Choose the correct conjunction that can combine the given sentences without changing their meaning.
 The children forgot their homework. The teacher was angry with them.
 (a) or   (b) so   (c) but   (d) if

30. Identify the adverb in the given sentence.
 You simply have to put one word in each space.
 (a) have to   (b) simply
 (c) put   (d) space

Directions (Q. Nos. 31-35) Read the poem and answer the questions that follow.

What if Batman ran when he saw a bat?
What kind of hero is afraid of that?
What if Aquaman was afraid of a shark?
Wouldn't that make him an easy mark?
If Spidey was afraid of spiders,
Would he still overcome the law's outsiders?
If the Joker couldn't tell a joke
Or Captain Cold's freeze ray was broke
If Poison Ivy's thumb wasn't green
Or if Lex Luthor wasn't mean
Comics wouldn't be much fun,
And I'd never get my reading done!

31. What is the speaker in the poem reading?
 (a) A taxtbook   (b) A poem
 (c) A comic book   (d) A storybook

32. What does the speaker think makes comics 'fun'?
 (a) The bravery of the heroes.
 (b) The good nature of the villains.
 (c) The battle between the heroes and the villains.
 (d) All of the above

33. How many rhyming pairs are there in the poem?
 (a) 3   (b) 5   (c) 4   (d) 6

34. "And I'd never get my reading done!" Who is 'I' in this line?
 (a) Spiderman   (b) Batman
 (c) Aquaman   (d) Poet

35. Choose the word from the passage which means opposite to 'nice'.
 (a) Mean   (b) Fun
 (c) Law   (d) Overcome

ANSWERS

Chapter 1   Noun

1. (b)	**2.** (d)	**3.** (a)	**4.** (c)	**5.** (c)	**6.** (b)	**7.** (a)	**8.** (b)	**9.** (c)	**10.** (c)
11. (d)	**12.** (c)	**13.** (b)	**14.** (b)	**15.** (c)	**16.** (d)	**17.** (c)	**18.** (d)	**19.** (c)	**20.** (b)
21. (c)	**22.** (c)	**23.** (b)	**24.** (b)	**25.** (c)	**26.** (c)	**27.** (b)	**28.** (a)	**29.** (b)	**30.** (c)

Chapter 2   Pronoun

1. (c)	**2.** (b)	**3.** (a)	**4.** (c)	**5.** (a)	**6.** (c)	**7.** (b)	**8.** (b)	**9.** (b)	**10.** (a)
11. (b)	**12.** (b)	**13.** (c)	**14.** (b)	**15.** (c)	**16.** (b)	**17.** (b)	**18.** (b)	**19.** (d)	**20.** (d)
21. (a)	**22.** (c)	**23.** (b)	**24.** (c)	**25.** (b)	**26.** (c)	**27.** (c)	**28.** (c)	**29.** (c)	**30.** (a)
31. (c)	**32.** (d)	**33.** (a)	**34.** (b)	**35.** (a)	**36.** (b)				

Chapter 3   Verb

1. (b)	**2.** (b)	**3.** (c)	**4.** (a)	**5.** (b)	**6.** (b)	**7.** (c)	**8.** (b)	**9.** (c)	**10.** (c)
11. (b)	**12.** (b)	**13.** (a)	**14.** (c)	**15.** (a)	**16.** (c)	**17.** (b)	**18.** (a)	**19.** (c)	**20.** (d)
21. (a)	**22.** (c)	**23.** (b)	**24.** (a)	**25.** (a)	**26.** (b)	**27.** (c)			

Chapter 4   Adverb

1. (b)	**2.** (c)	**3.** (d)	**4.** (a)	**5.** (d)	**6.** (c)	**7.** (c)	**8.** (b)	**9.** (b)	**10.** (a)
11. (b)	**12.** (a)	**13.** (d)	**14.** (b)	**15.** (a)	**16.** (d)	**17.** (c)	**18.** (b)	**19.** (b)	**20.** (c)
21. (c)	**22.** (b)	**23.** (a)	**24.** (d)	**25.** (c)	**26.** (b)	**27.** (a)	**28.** (d)	**29.** (b)	**30.** (d)
31. (d)									

Chapter 5   Adjective

1. (c)	**2.** (c)	**3.** (b)	**4.** (b)	**5.** (b)	**6.** (d)	**7.** (b)	**8.** (a)	**9.** (d)	**10.** (d)
11. (c)	**12.** (c)	**13.** (c)	**14.** (d)	**15.** (c)	**16.** (c)	**17.** (d)	**18.** (d)	**19.** (a)	**20.** (b)
21. (b)	**22.** (d)	**23.** (a)	**24.** (b)	**25.** (b)					

Chapter 6   Article

1. (a)	**2.** (c)	**3.** (b)	**4.** (a)	**5.** (c)	**6.** (b)	**7.** (b)	**8.** (c)	**9.** (a)	**10.** (d)
11. (b)	**12.** (a)	**13.** (a)	**14.** (c)	**15.** (c)	**16.** (a)	**17.** (b)	**18.** (a)	**19.** (b)	**20.** (d)
21. (c)	**22.** (b)	**23.** (a)	**24.** (d)	**25.** (c)					

Chapter 7   Prepositions

1. (b)	**2.** (c)	**3.** (a)	**4.** (a)	**5.** (c)	**6.** (c)	**7.** (a)	**8.** (c)	**9.** (c)	**10.** (c)
11. (c)	**12.** (c)	**13.** (a)	**14.** (b)	**15.** (d)	**16.** (c)	**17.** (d)	**18.** (d)	**19.** (d)	**20.** (c)
21. (b)	**22.** (a)	**23.** (c)	**24.** (d)	**25.** (a)	**26.** (c)	**27.** (b)	**28.** (c)	**29.** (c)	**30.** (b)
31. (c)	**32.** (d)	**33.** (b)	**34.** (c)	**35.** (b)	**36.** (b)	**37.** (c)	**38.** (a)	**39.** (b)	**40.** (a)

Chapter 8   Conjunctions

1. (c)	2. (d)	3. (b)	4. (b)	5. (a)	6. (c)	7. (c)	8. (c)	9. (b)	10. (c)
11. (c)	12. (c)	13. (a)	14. (d)	15. (a)	16. (d)	17. (c)	18. (b)	19. (d)	20. (b)
21. (b)	22. (d)	23. (b)	24. (a)	25. (d)	26. (b)	27. (c)	28. (a)	29. (b)	30. (b)

Chapter 9   Sentence and Its Types

1. (b)	2. (c)	3. (a)	4. (b)	5. (c)	6. (b)	7. (d)	8. (b)	9. (b)	10. (b)
11. (c)	12. (b)	13. (b)	14. (b)	15. (b)	16. (c)	17. (b)	18. (c)	19. (b)	20. (c)
21. (b)	22. (c)	23. (b)	24. (a)	25. (a)	26. (c)	27. (a)	28. (b)		

Chapter 10   Tense

1. (b)	2. (b)	3. (a)	4. (c)	5. (b)	6. (c)	7. (c)	8. (c)	9. (d)	10. (a)
11. (b)	12. (a)	13. (c)	14. (c)	15. (b)	16. (a)	17. (c)	18. (d)	19. (c)	20. (b)
21. (b)	22. (c)	23. (a)	24. (a)	25. (c)	26. (c)				

Chapter 11   Punctuation

1. (b)	2. (a)	3. (c)	4. (a)	5. (b)	6. (d)	7. (c)	8. (b)	9. (c)	10. (d)
11. (b)	12. (c)	13. (d)	14. (b)	15. (c)	16. (b)	17. (b)	18. (c)	19. (a)	20. (d)
21. (d)	22. (a)	23. (b)	24. (b)	25. (d)	26. (d)	27. (c)	28. (c)	29. (c)	30. (b)

Chapter 12   Jumbled Words and Sentences

1. (b)	2. (c)	3. (b)	4. (d)	5. (c)	6. (c)	7. (d)	8. (b)	9. (b)	10. (b)
11. (c)	12. (d)	13. (b)	14. (b)	15. (d)	16. (c)	17. (b)	18. (c)	19. (a)	20. (d)
21. (b)	22. (a)	23. (b)	24. (b)	25. (c)	26. (a)	27. (d)	28. (a)	29. (d)	30. (c)
31. (a)	32. (c)	33. (b)	34. (b)	35. (c)	36. (a)	37. (d)	38. (d)	39. (b)	40. (d)

Chapter 13   Synonyms

1. (d)	2. (b)	3. (c)	4. (d)	5. (b)	6. (d)	7. (b)	8. (c)	9. (d)	10. (c)
11. (c)	12. (d)	13. (c)	14. (b)	15. (a)	16. (d)	17. (a)	18. (c)	19. (b)	20. (d)
21. (c)	22. (a)	23. (c)	24. (b)	25. (c)	26. (b)	27. (b)	28. (c)	29. (c)	30. (a)
31. (b)	32. (c)	33. (b)	34. (a)	35. (a)					

Chapter 14   Antonyms

1. (d)	2. (b)	3. (a)	4. (d)	5. (a)	6. (d)	7. (c)	8. (c)	9. (d)	10. (b)
11. (a)	12. (c)	13. (b)	14. (d)	15. (b)	16. (c)	17. (a)	18. (d)	19. (c)	20. (b)
21. (d)	22. (d)	23. (c)	24. (d)	25. (b)	26. (a)	27. (c)	28. (d)	29. (a)	30. (c)
31. (b)	32. (c)	33. (a)	34. (b)	35. (d)					

Chapter 15   Word Pair/Word Analogy

1. (a)	2. (b)	3. (c)	4. (d)	5. (c)	6. (c)	7. (b)	8. (b)	9. (c)	10. (d)
11. (b)	12. (a)	13. (d)	14. (c)	15. (b)	16. (a)	17. (d)	18. (c)	19. (b)	20. (d)
21. (c)	22. (a)	23. (d)	24. (d)	25. (c)	26. (a)	27. (c)	28. (d)	29. (b)	30. (c)
31. (d)	32. (b)	33. (a)	34. (c)	35. (b)	36. (a)	37. (d)	38. (b)	39. (b)	40. (b)

Chapter 16   Spelling Test

1. (c)	2. (b)	3. (a)	4. (d)	5. (c)	6. (a)	7. (c)	8. (d)	9. (b)	10. (a)
11. (a)	12. (b)	13. (b)	14. (a)	15. (d)	16. (c)	17. (a)	18. (c)	19. (b)	20. (d)
21. (a)	22. (c)	23. (a)	24. (d)	25. (b)	26. (c)	27. (c)	28. (a)	29. (d)	30. (b)
31. (c)	32. (d)	33. (b)	34. (a)	35. (d)					

Chapter 17   Idioms and Phrases

1. (b)	2. (a)	3. (c)	4. (b)	5. (a)	6. (a)	7. (c)	8. (c)	9. (d)	10. (a)
11. (c)	12. (a)	13. (b)	14. (c)	15. (d)	16. (d)	17. (b)	18. (c)	19. (d)	20. (a)
21. (c)	22. (b)	23. (a)	24. (c)	25. (d)					

Chapter 18   One Word Substitution

1. (c)	2. (d)	3. (d)	4. (b)	5. (a)	6. (c)	7. (b)	8. (c)	9. (b)	10. (a)
11. (b)	12. (a)	13. (d)	14. (a)	15. (c)	16. (b)	17. (a)	18. (d)	19. (a)	20. (b)
21. (b)	22. (c)	23. (a)	24. (d)	25. (b)					

Chapter 19   Reading Comprehension

Passage 1	1. (b)	2. (c)	3. (c)	4. (c)	5. (c)	**Poem 1**	16. (d)	17. (c)	18. (b)	19. (a)	20. (d)
Passage 2	6. (b)	7. (c)	8. (b)	9. (b)	10. (c)	**Poem 2**	21. (b)	22. (a)	23. (d)	24. (b)	25. (c)
Passage 3	11. (a)	12. (d)	13. (c)	14. (a)	15. (c)	**Poem 3**	26. (b)	27. (a)	28. (b)	29. (c)	30. (c)

Chapter 20   Spoken and Written Expression

1. (b)	2. (d)	3. (b)	4. (c)	5. (b)	6. (d)	7. (a)	8. (b)	9. (c)	10. (d)
11. (a)	12. (b)	13. (c)	14. (d)	15. (c)	16. (b)	17. (b)	18. (c)	19. (a)	20. (d)

Practice Set 1

1. (c)	2. (d)	3. (c)	4. (d)	5. (b)	6. (a)	7. (d)	8. (a)	9. (b)	10. (c)
11. (b)	12. (d)	13. (d)	14. (a)	15. (b)	16. (c)	17. (d)	18. (c)	19. (d)	20. (c)
21. (c)	22. (d)	23. (b)	24. (a)	25. (d)	26. (c)	27. (a)	28. (c)	29. (d)	30. (a)
31. (c)	32. (d)	33. (b)	34. (a)	35. (c)					

Practice Set 2

1. (d)	2. (c)	3. (c)	4. (c)	5. (b)	6. (b)	7. (b)	8. (c)	9. (d)	10. (b)
11. (d)	12. (c)	13. (c)	14. (a)	15. (b)	16. (d)	17. (b)	18. (d)	19. (d)	20. (b)
21. (a)	22. (c)	23. (d)	24. (a)	25. (c)	26. (a)	27. (b)	28. (c)	29. (b)	30. (b)
31. (c)	32. (a)	33. (d)	34. (d)	35. (a)					